AMERICAN
FILMMAKERS
TODAY

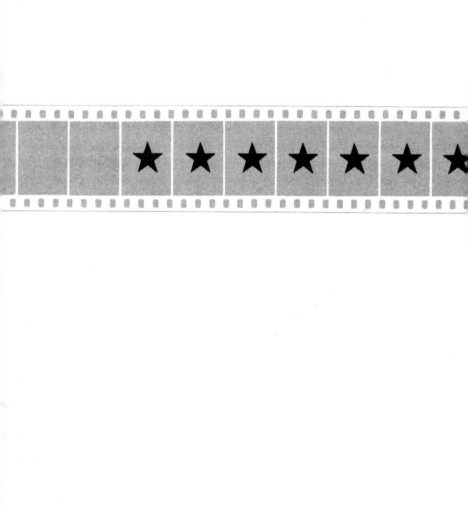

AMERICAN ★ FILMMAKERS TODAY

Dian G. Smith

BLANDFORD PRESS
POOLE · DORSET

First published in the UK 1984 by
Blandford Press, Link House, West Street,
Poole, Dorset, BH15 1LL

First published in the USA
1983 by Julian Messner
A Division of Simon & Schuster, Inc.
Simon & Schuster Building
1230 Avenue of the Americas,
New York, New York 10020

British Library Cataloguing in Publication Data

Smith, Dian G.
  American film makers today.
  1. Moving-pictures—United States—History
  I. Title
  791.43'0973   PN1993.5.U6

ISBN 0 7137 1519 7 (hardback)
     0 7137 1520 0 (paperback)

Designed by Prairie Graphics·

Printed and bound in Great Britain by
Mackays of Chatham Ltd., Kent

Acknowledgments

I am very grateful for the excellent film study collections of the Library of the Performing Arts (the New York Public Library at Lincoln Center) and the Museum of Modern Art in New York City, and for the great research library of Columbia University.

At Julian Messner, I would like to thank my editor, Jane Steltenpohl, who launched me on this project and provided wise criticism and guidance.

I must also thank Robert S. Smith, supporter, critic, and movie companion; Benjamin Eli and Emlen Matthew Smith, experts on *Star Wars*; and Marie-Nicole Exantus, the most skilled and loving baby-sitter.

ALSO BY DIAN G. SMITH
Careers in the Visual Arts
Talking with Professionals

Contents

Introduction

IN THE HEYDAY of Hollywood, directors (like actors) were hired hands, working under contract for one or another of the six major studios. They were kept busy churning out pictures to be shown on double bills in the studios' theater chains. Today the situation in Hollywood is very different.

The change began in 1948, when the Supreme Court ruled, under the antitrust laws, that the connection between the studios and the theaters was a monopoly. During the 1950s the studios were forced to sell their theaters. Without these guaranteed outlets, the risk in financing and producing films greatly increased (the average Hollywood movie today costs $10 million). At the same time, television was drawing audiences away, and the new suburban life-style was keeping families more often together at home. The studios had to cut back and began to rely on independent production companies to make many of their films, which they would then only distribute.

What this has meant for directors, in part, is a loss of security. But it has also meant, for some, the opportunity to do more than direct a film, to become what is often called a "filmmaker." A filmmaker has control over the film from conception through release—originating the idea, writing the screenplay, and then directing, producing, and perhaps acting in and marketing the film (or some influential combination of these).

The nine directors whose stories are told in this book took that opportunity. They are filmmakers who have used their total control to convey some vision of their own, to make personal films. Yet they walk a fine line between art and commerce. They were granted control of their films primarily because they can attract long enough lines to the box office to satisfy the studios.

A number of other filmmakers might have been included in this book—Hal Ashby, John Cassavetes, Terrence Malick, and Michael Ritchie, for instance. And among those chosen, some might consider George Lucas's films too commercial or Robert Altman's too personal. The intent was to find directors whose stated aim is to make personal films, who made their major films in the 1970s, and who seem likely to be making more in the 1980s. Ultimately, of course, any selection is a matter of personal judgment.

This book is limited to Hollywood directors because Hollywood films are the ones that most people see. In this country there is also a thriving underground of personal filmmakers whose films are distributed independently. They are sometimes bought by studios, but more often are distributed through less commercial outlets (art theaters, universities, museums, festivals).

The future for personal filmmakers in America is hard to predict, for the 1980s, like the 1950s, promise to be years of change in Hollywood. Cable TV, videocassettes, and other new technologies could provide a huge, hungry market for films. If so, a book on this subject published ten years from now might have twice as many names, including, one hopes, those of some women and some blacks.

Woody Allen

WHO IS WOODY ALLEN? Is he the brainy nebbish of the nightclub acts and the early films, panting after women and terrorized by anything mechanical? Or is he Sandy Bates of *Stardust Memories*, the tormented filmmaker whose boorish fans won't allow him to express his concerns in serious films? Or is he someone else entirely?

In the first place, Woody Allen was not always Woody Allen. He was born Allen Stewart Konigsberg on December 1, 1935, in Flatbush, a lower-middle-class neighborhood in Brooklyn. And contrary to his weakling image, his father claims that he was

1

Woody Allen directing *A Midsummer Night's Sex Comedy*.

dubbed Woody by the kids on the block because he was always the one to bring the stick out for the stickball game. Woody also trained to be a featherweight fighter and would have entered the Golden Gloves if his father hadn't refused to sign the papers for him.

Woody's parents were poor, and when he was young they often lived with relatives because of the wartime housing shortage. His father held various jobs while Woody was growing up, including taxi driver and waiter, until he opened his own business as a jewelry engraver. His mother was a bookkeeper in a florist shop.

Woody and his younger sister Letty were raised as Orthodox Jews, and he went to Hebrew school for eight years. He isn't religious now, though, and was less than reverent even then. His father told an interviewer that at his bar mitzvah Woody put on blackface and did Al Jolson's jazz singer routine.

Although he made his parents the butt of some of his jokes ("Their values in life are God and carpeting," he used to say on the stage), he is actually fond of them and visits them regularly. And Letty is always one of the early viewers of his films.

As a child, Woody was shy and not very popular. He made fun of the bullying he suffered then in a nightclub joke about his stay at an interfaith camp: "I was sadistically beaten by boys of all races and creeds."

In general, Allen has described his childhood as "classic low-brow." He spent his time playing ball, watching wrestling on television, and reading comic books and Mickey Spillane novels. He also went to the Flatbush Theater five times a week, where he saw "vaudeville and movies and . . . every comic, every tap dancer, every magician, every kind of singer. . . . I could do everybody's act. I used to tear up the Raisinets boxes and write jokes down."

At the age of seven he saw Bob Hope in *The Road to Monaco* and decided that he wanted to be a comedian. Hope has remained an idol. "I feel I have characteristics in common with

Hope," he has said. "We're both cowards, womanizers, egotistical, vain. He was not a clown in the sense of Chaplin or Keaton. He was the guy next door, the man from the electric company. You really believed him." In 1979 Allen prepared a selection from Hope's films titled "My Favorite Comedian" for a public tribute. He said at that time that Hope's influence "appears throughout my work."

At thirteen, Woody became obsessed with magic (like Paul in his play *The Floating Lightbulb*) and would spend three or four hours a day teaching himself card tricks.

At fifteen, he fell in love with jazz and bought a soprano saxophone, which he taught himself to play. Later he switched to the clarinet. He still practices along with records at least an hour a day and plays once a week with a band at Michael's Pub in New York City.

Allen said of himself as a child, "Although I never laughed out loud then, I was a funny kid. My viewpoint was funny, and I said funny things." At the suggestion of a relative, he wrote some of those funny things down and sent them in to newspaper columnists under an assumed name. One that appeared in an Earl Wilson column was: "Woody Allen boasts that he just made a fortune downtown—he auctioned off his parking space."

The publication of these jokes led to a part-time job after school at a public relations firm. For two years he produced fifty gags a day to be used by the firm's clients. He was paid $25 a week. "I was utterly thrilled by the job," he said. "I thought I was in the heart of show business."

He was less thrilled about school. Although his compositions were always the ones read aloud in class, he graduated from high school with a 71 average. To satisfy his parents, Allen enrolled in college—twice. Both times he flunked out in his freshman year and went to work instead writing for comedians. At nineteen, he became a full-time NBC staff writer. He also got married that year to a girl he had known since high school. The marriage didn't work—they were both too young, he said—and they got divorced five years later.

Meanwhile Allen started seeing a psychoanalyst: "I was very unhappy. No particular reason, just a feeling I couldn't shake." He still goes to an analyst, sometimes as often as five times a week. Friends have described him as suffering from feelings of guilt, anger, and shame. He is also very self-critical. "I'm surprised at the amount of people that go to see my films," he has said. "All of my films have been personal failures," falling far short of "the grandiose plan I had in mind."

But Allen's personal problems have not stood in the way of his professional success. "I never get so depressed that it interferes with my work. I can go into a room every morning and churn it out."

By 1962 Woody Allen was one of the highest-paid writers in television comedy. Then his manager persuaded him to perform his lines on stage himself. "That took more courage than I knew I had," he said. "When I . . . decided to be a writer . . . it was in part because I was terrified of dealing with people, and I wanted to remain isolated. So it was an enormous wrench for me to go from the most ideally isolated situation to the most public situation available." He still prefers writing to either performing or directing.

According to his manager, Allen was "awful" at first: "Of course, he had good lines. But he was so scared and embarrassed and—rabbity. If you gave him an excuse not to go on, he'd take it." Two years later, however, Allen was earning $5,000 a week in well-known nightclubs, had made a record, and was a popular guest star on television comedy shows.

Although it hadn't taken him long to gain confidence on the stage, Allen still filled his act with stammers and hesitations—all carefully timed. Talking mainly about himself, he conveyed a sense of exclusion and inadequacy, of the little man against the elements. Of his wife he would frequently say, "We'd always have these deep philosophical discussions, and she always proved I didn't exist." He was so poor, he said, that he had a pet ant named Spot.

He had a phenomenal rapport with audiences. The critic Richard Schickel wrote, "All of us watching him, whatever our sizes or shapes, harbored a Woody Allen inside ourselves." Many viewers of his films, in which he usually stars, have the same feeling. But it would be wrong to assume that Woody Allen's real personality is the same as his stage personality. Although his clothes are the same onstage and off—beat-up sports jacket, open plaid sports shirts, loose pants—the effect is quite different.

Woody Allen is never "on" when he is not acting. He is an extremely hardworking, very private, shy man. His schedule, when he is not directing a film, is to get up at seven o'clock, write all day, and then go out for a late dinner with a few close friends. He doesn't drink, smoke, or take drugs. On meeting him for the first time, the film critic Janet Maslin wrote, "I was surprised to find him so solemn, so adult, so composed, so controlled, so unneurotic." And he has said of himself, "I'm preoccupied with problems and work, and I'm certainly not the delight of any party."

Interviewers are also surprised at the elegance of his home. He lives in a magnificent duplex penthouse apartment furnished in the style of a French country house. It overlooks New York's Central Park, and some of the opening scenes of his film *Manhattan* were shot from his terrace.

While Allen was winning acclaim as a stand-up comic, he also started contributing humorous essays to the *New Yorker* and other magazines. He still writes these pieces, which have been published in several collections. They are satires on language and culture, dealing with subjects as different as organized crime and philosophers and with titles like "If the Impressionists Had Been Dentists." Although he has claimed that he just tosses these off, his editor at the *New Yorker* described him as "a marvel of a willing and hardworking writer."

Woody Allen's goal at the beginning of his career, however,

was to be a playwright, and before he ever directed a film he had had two Broadway successes: *Don't Drink the Water* (1966) and *Play It Again, Sam* (1969).

Don't Drink the Water is about a Newark caterer who, while touring with his wife and daughter in an Eastern European country, gets into trouble for photographing a secret military installation. The play includes an Allen-like character who wins the girl after various bungling attempts to help. The play got mixed reviews: some critics complained that it was just a collection of one-liners. Allen claimed that he never intended it to be a classical play, but rather "the kind of very broad thing the Marx Brothers did. What fascinated me was the old formless farce." In any case, audiences liked it, and it played on Broadway for eighteen months.

Allen described his second Broadway comedy, *Play It Again, Sam*, as "an autobiographical story about a highly neurotic lover—an accumulation of themes that interest me: sex, adultery, extreme neuroses in romance, insecurity." Allan Felix (originally played by Allen himself) is a film critic whose wife has left him in bad shape: he can't even cook TV dinners; he sucks them frozen. (The play coincided with the breakup after three years of Allen's second marriage to Louise Lasser, who later won fame as Mary Hartman on television.)

Felix tries to model himself on Humphrey Bogart in order to make a new conquest. After several catastrophes, he falls in love with his best friend's wife (played by Diane Keaton, with whom Allen was having a romance in real life). Again, the play was not a critical success. "It is stringed with jokes, some hilarious, but it is not a play," wrote drama critic Walter Kerr. And again, audiences loved it, and it ran for more than a year.

Play It Again, Sam was made into a film in 1972. Although Allen wrote the screenplay and peformed in it, he chose an old pro, Herbert Ross, to direct. "I would never want to direct a play into a movie," he said. "I would only be interested in working on original projects for the screen."

No other Woody Allen plays were produced until *The Floating Lightbulb*, in 1981. It is the story of a poor Jewish family in Brooklyn in 1945, and a terribly shy boy who dreams of being a magician. Allen described it as a "modest little play," and critics, used to his adventurous filmmaking by this time, were disappointed that, as Frank Rich put it in the *New York Times*, "as a serious playwright, Mr. Allen is still learning his craft and finding his voice."

Woody Allen made his film debut not in his own movie but in *What's New, Pussycat?* (1965), a slapstick bedroom farce. He wrote the screenplay as "a Marx Brothers kind of script" and played the role of an undresser in a strip club. The stars, Peter Sellers and Peter O'Toole, changed the script, and Allen said of the film, "I never considered that one mine. I hated it, I hated making it, and it was the reason I became a director." Although *Pussycat* was panned by the critics, it was a box office hit, and it brought Woody Allen national fame.

His next project was *What's Up, Tiger Lily?* (1966). He and a group of friends improvised a comic English sound track for a cheaply made Japanese spy thriller. Phil Moscowitz (a Japanese actor with Allen's voice) and his allies and enemies are on a violent quest, for "it is written that he who has the best recipe for egg salad shall rule over heaven and earth." Most critics found the dialogue funny but thought that the joke didn't deserve a whole film. Allen himself hated the film and sued to stop its release. Other actors added jokes he said were "stupid," and his voice was dubbed in places.

Allen then performed in a second film for the producer of *Pussycat*. This one was *Casino Royale* (1967), a James Bond spoof. Allen was cast against type as Jimmy, Bond's nephew, a tough superspy. Most of his scenes were monologues, and he ad-libbed more than half his lines. "I never bothered to see *Casino Royale*," he said. "I knew it would be a horrible film. The set was a chaotic madhouse. I knew then that the only way to make a film is to control it completely."

Allen worked only once more as a hired hand, starring in a serious film, *The Front* (1976). He played a wisecracking, slightly neurotic loser who becomes involved in investigations during the McCarthy era because he acted as a front for blacklisted TV writers. "I didn't look at *The Front* as my chance to play Hamlet," Allen said at the time. "The reason I did *The Front* was that the subject was worthwhile."

Woody Allen's career as a filmmaker began in earnest in 1969 with *Take the Money and Run*. Since then he has had complete control of his films from conception through opening. He oversees the credits, the ads, and the theaters where the movies play, as well as making every artistic decision.

In all his films, Allen has tended to cast people he knows and trusts (former wives, friends, and lovers like Louise Lasser, Tony Roberts, and Diane Keaton). He has said that he does this because he is shy. His collaborations on scripts, also with friends, have involved what Marshall Brickman (coauthor of two films) described as "highly stylized conversations"—talking and talking and talking and then remembering what was good and putting it down on paper.

Allen allows his actors to improvise and shoots much more footage than he can use. His direction, he has said, "consists usually of 'faster,' 'louder,' and 'more real.'" But the atmosphere on his sets is not relaxed. Gene Wilder, who played a successful doctor who leaves his wife for a sheep named Daisy in a segment of *Everything You Always Wanted to Know about Sex*, described the set of that movie as "people talking in whispers, serious looks on Woody's face. He communicates through silence."

Woody Allen's first five films—from *Take the Money and Run* through *Love and Death*—are what he has called "comedy that was strictly for laughs." Although they become progressively more skillful, they have a certain style in common. Their composition is purely functional, the gags are more important than the narrative, the camera is tied down, and the movie is made with cuts.

In 1974, he said, "The closest analogy to my films would be the Tom and Jerry cartoons. A guy runs out and you smash him on the head with something and he doesn't die and he doesn't bleed and it's past and you clear the decks for the next joke right away." These films all received good reviews and were reasonably successful at the box office, although his urban humor was most popular in big cities.

The first film, *Take the Money and Run*, Allen has said, was "strictly a learning experience." It is a mock documentary, which he wrote with his high-school friend Mickey Rose. In a series of short, funny sketches he documents the inept criminal history of Virgil Starkwell (Allen), "known to police in six states for assault, armed robbery, and possession of a wart," as the earnest narrator relates. In one sketch the gun he carves out of soap and blackens with shoe polish for his prison break dissolves in the rain.

In *Bananas* (also written with Mickey Rose), he is more experimental. He parodies several scenes from famous films and also moves his characters out of New York. Allen plays Fielding Melish, an apolitical products tester whose products tend to attack him. He somehow becomes the leader of a revolution in South America in the course of trying to impress Nancy, a fashionably liberal girl (played by Louise Lasser). *Bananas* begins and ends with an appearance by Howard Cosell, being himself. At first he is commenting in the midst of a political coup; then he is ringside on the eve of Fielding's marriage to Nancy. In this film, too, Allen has said, his method was "to have a thin story line to hang the comedy sequences on."

Everything You Always Wanted to Know about Sex is "the first picture where I've cared about anything but the jokes. I wanted to do something where the color was really pretty and controlled, and the moves contributed and everything worked." In each of the seven episodes, based on questions in the popular sex manual, Allen parodies a type of film or television program and experiments with color and sets. Although critics found some episodes tasteless or tedious, almost all agreed that "What Happens during Ejaculation?" is brilliant. The scene takes place inside the male body, at a NASA-like headquarters, where Allen plays a cowardly sperm.

The idea for *Sleeper* came from this successful episode. *Sleeper* is a science fiction satire about the operator of a health food store who goes into the hospital for an ulcer operation in the 1970s and wakes up after two hundred years of frozen animation. The world he finds is ruled by a voice coming from the television set. All needs are filled by robots and machines, like the silver ball that can be rubbed for instant pleasure ("even worse than California," he says). Allen wrote the script with Marshall Brickman, who had written jokes for his nightclub act in the sixties.

With this film Allen makes a slight shift in style. He uses more physical comedy and pantomime, and the humor is based more on a concept than on basically unconnected gags. He uses the framework of the future to comment on sophisticated modern life. In *Sleeper*, also, he has said, "I became aware of visuals. Since then, I've gotten deeper and deeper into visually arresting films."

Love and Death is another good-looking film, shot in "soft, autumnal colors." This time he uses the past (nineteenth-century Russia) as his framework. Boris Grushenko (Allen), a "militant coward," tells the story of his life, including his fateful wavering over the decision to kill Napoleon: "If I don't kill him he'll make war all through Europe. But murder . . . What would Socrates say?" He later ponders his death before a firing squad: "There are worse things in life than death," he says the night before. The film also tells of Boris's passion for his pseudointellectual cousin Sonia (Diane Keaton), who gets him into this mess.

Allen has said that *Love and Death* makes a "slight satirical point about dying, and war, and the transitory quality of love." He has also said that "the serious intent underlying the humor was not very apparent to most audiences. Laughter submerges

Woody Allen and Diane Keaton in a scene from *Annie Hall*. PHOTO: United Press International

everything else. That's why I felt that, with *Annie Hall*, I would have to reduce some of the laughter. I didn't want to destroy the credibility for the sake of the laugh."

Annie Hall, his next film, led the way to a series of films that are more human and less like cartoons. It is the story of a love affair, told through the drifting recollections of Alvy Singer (Allen), a melancholy, self-critical comedy writer. It is a film about relationships, not a farce. In the opening monologue Alvy says, "Annie and I broke up." And he asks, "Where did the screw-up come?" *Annie Hall* has some funny anecdotes and one-liners, but there are fewer of them and they are tied more closely to the characters. For example, the hilarious scene where Alvy and Annie chase their live lobster dinner around the kitchen (he suggests luring it from behind the refrigerator with butter sauce) occurs while they are getting to know each other.

The Allen character in this film is more complex than ever before and has real feelings. When he goes to California to try to get back the now sun-tanned, self-assured Annie, he feels sad and insecure.

Of the change from the earlier films to *Annie Hall*, Allen said at the time: "In order to grow, I knew I'd have to deepen the work—to use comedy in the service of ideas, or more genuine satire, or emotional exploration. It's an attempt to develop."

In this film he also develops his style as a filmmaker. The camera is allowed to move, and there is a deliberate three-color scheme: the romantic New York scenes were shot on overcast days or at sundown; scenes from the past have a nostalgic, golden-yellow hue; and the California scenes were shot right into the sun so that people almost seem to evaporate. He uses a split screen, animation, instant replay, and even subtitles in a scene where Alvy is looking at Annie's photographs:

ALVY: They're wonderful, you know. They have a quality.

(*SUBTITLE:* You are a great-looking girl.)
ANNIE: Well, I would like to take a serious photography
          course.
(*SUBTITLE:* He probably thinks I'm a yo-yo.)

Although Allen claims that *Annie Hall* is a work of fiction, the main character, like Allen, is a writer and also, like Allen, has a relationship with Diane Keaton (whose real last name is Hall). The film also reflects Allen's feeling of being a Jew in a Protestant world. (On first meeting Alvy, Annie exclaims, "You're what Grammy Hall would call a real Jew!") And it is flavored with some of his favorite prejudices, including his dislike of California. "I can't live in any city where the only cultural advantage is that you can make a right turn on a red light," says Alvy.

Annie Hall was a hit. It won four Oscars—for screenplay (written with Marshall Brickman), direction, best picture, and best actress (Diane Keaton). It won the New York and National Film Critics awards, a Directors Guild award, and raves from the major American critics. But Allen remained unsatisfied: "*Annie Hall*, to me, was a very middle-class picture, and that's why I think people liked it. It was the reinforcement of middle-class values."

Allen decided to make his next film a "serious" one. As early as 1968 he had been naming Ingmar Bergman as the filmmaker who most influenced him: "Bergman interests me more than anyone because of the consummate marriage of technique, theatricality, and themes that are both personally important to me and that have gigantic size—death, the meaning of life, the question of religious faith." He said of his serious film while he was making it—as if anticipating the criticism—"I'm feeling my way, just as when I was beginning as a cabaret comedian. I have to watch out for touches of other people in my work."

Interiors, the only one of his films in which Woody Allen does not appear, is a psychological drama about a genteel New England family—a controlling mother, a distant father, and three unhappy daughters. One of them, Renata, a talented and successful poet played by Diane Keaton, Allen said, "articulates all my personal concerns. . . . You have a sense of immortality that your work will live on after you, which is nonsense. . . . Renata comes to realize in the movie . . . that the only thing anyone has any chance with is human relationships."

Like *Annie Hall*, this film is about how and why relationships fail, but it has a much graver tone. Allen's directorial style changed, too. "I was always telling them to play smaller, don't do so much . . . whereas in a comedy film, it's always louder and faster."

Interiors split the critics into two camps: many found it a pretentious attempt to copy Bergman; others admired it. Allen was nominated for an Academy Award as best director.

With his next film, Woody Allen bounced back firmly into the critics' good graces, winning the New York Film Critics Circle award for best director. *Manhattan* (again written with Marshall Brickman) returned to the romantic comedy style of *Annie Hall*. Allen said about the film, "I wanted to make an amusing film, but a film with feelings that went deeper than *Annie Hall*."

Manhattan is a straight narrative about Isaac Davis (Allen), a successful TV writer who leaves his job to write a serious novel. The film portrays his relationships with seventeen-year-old Tracy ("I'm going out with a girl who does homework," he mocks himself) and Mary (Diane Keaton), a neurotic writer and the mistress of his married best friend Yale (Tony Roberts). It deals, in his words, with the problem of trying "to live a decent life amid all the junk of contemporary culture—the temptations, the seductions."

Allen intended *Manhattan* to be "a metaphor for everything wrong with our culture." And there is much that is wrong with the slick, upper-class New York people of this film, where Mary makes pretentious comments about art, Yale broods deeply over buying a Porsche, and Isaac tries to run over his former wife's female lover.

The film is visually sophisticated. Shot in black and white, it uses compositions with depth and shadow. Richard Schickel, in *Time* magazine, called it "the perfect blending of style and substance, humor and humanity."

Stardust Memories, Allen's next film, though also a comic drama, stirred some of the same controversy as *Interiors*. It is the story of Sandy Bates (Allen), a filmmaker attending a weekend film seminar on his own films at the Hotel Stardust. He doesn't want to make comedies anymore but his vulgar, fawning fans criticize him for his recent seriousness. This time Allen was accused of copying Fellini, whose 8½ is about a director at an artistic and spiritual impasse. *Stardust Memories* is filled with ideas about comedy, suffering celebrity, and the search for the right woman.

Although Woody Allen insisted that it was wrong to identify Sandy Bates with himself, many critics and audiences felt his hostility directed at them in the film.

A *Midsummer Night's Sex Comedy*, released two years later, has none of the bitterness of *Stardust Memories*, but it lacks the comic spirit of his other films. It is about the romantic intermingling of three couples in a country house at the turn of the century. Among them are a Wall Street broker and crackpot inventor (Allen), a lady-killing doctor (Tony Roberts), and a worldly femme fatale (Mia Farrow, Allen's current girl friend in real life). Critics described the film as "amiable" and "pretty" and "entertaining," but almost always as "slight."

They used only superlatives for his next film, however, several critics hailing *Zelig* as Allen's best and wittiest. *Zelig* is a mock-documentary like *Take the Money and Run*, but much smoother and surer. It recounts the life of Leonard Zelig (Allen), supposedly a national figure of the 1920s and 30s. Newspapers dub him "the chameleon man" because he takes on the physical and mental characteristics of those around him, from black jazz musicians to bearded rabbis. Mia Farrow plays Dr. Eudora Fletcher, a psychiatrist who solemnly dedicates herself to curing Zelig and ends up falling in love with him.

The story is told through old newsreels blended perfectly with new material. Allen fits convincingly among the entourages of both Pope Pius XI and Adolf Hitler. There is commentary on his historical significance by modern intellectuals like Susan Sontag and footage of his sessions with Dr. Fletcher during which he becomes a psychiatrist himself. He is treating two pairs of Siamese twins with split personalities, he tells her. "I receive fees from eight people."

Allen has finished another film, *Broadway Danny Rose*, which will be released in early 1984. It was kept under tight cover before and during production, as are all his films, and there is no way to guess what it will be like. Allen has said, "There is a tendency among comedians to hit on something the public likes and then just grind it out for the rest of their lives. . . . I want to write all sorts of things. . . ."

Robert Altman with Lauren Bacall during the filming of *Health*. PHOTO: United Press International

Robert Altman

ROBERT ALTMAN has had only two real commercial successes—*M*A*S*H* and *Nashville*—and his films are almost always controversial. They are called poetical and pretentious, masterpieces and mishmashes. Altman himself is also controversial. A large, commanding man, he has infuriated and bewildered studio heads by insisting on doing things his own way. Yet most critics and serious filmgoers regard Robert Altman as an important filmmaker. He has directed films with a personal style, and he has directed many of them—fifteen since *M*A*S*H*, his antiwar black comedy (not to be confused with the television series), which made him the hottest director of 1970.

When he became Hollywood's whiz kid, Robert Altman was no kid at all. He was forty-five years old. "I think that if I'd done *M*A*S*H* when I was thirty-two," he said, "I'd be a hack today. I think if I'd gotten that much adulation I would have become very cocky." Instead he spent those thirteen years on the outskirts of the film industry, directing industrial films for corporations and episodes for television series.

Robert Altman was born on February 20, 1925, in Kansas City, Missouri, the oldest of three children. His father was a very successful insurance salesman and a habitual gambler. Altman also is a gambler and even made a film on the subject, *California Split* ("a celebration of gambling," he called it). To him, gambling is not a sin or a disease; it provides "the excitement of being near danger."

Altman describes his upbringing as "normal" and "uneventful," and his family as "very American, commercially oriented" people. For the conservative old-money family of his film *A Wedding*, he drew on his own. "All my aunts sang, or played the harp, and they'd all gone to Europe, and spoke French." He named the movie family's matriarch "Nettie" after his grandmother.

Not a good student, though talented in math and drawing, Altman majored in mathematical engineering at the University of Missouri. But he dropped out and joined the army at eighteen, when he also abandoned the Catholicism he had grown up with.

As a child, Altman has said, "I just loved the movies. I saw them all, went all the time." Once he played hooky from school in order to see *Viva Villa!* with Wallace Beery. He entered the theater at noon and didn't emerge until nine o'clock that night, when his parents dragged him out. Another time, when he had the mumps, he climbed out his window to see *King Kong*.

Altman has said that the most important influences on him were the directors of the films he saw in his childhood—especially Howard Hawks and John Huston. He also remembers discovering the English films of the forties; Fellini's *La Dolce Vita*; and Bergman's films, especially *Persona*. "But the best film I've seen *ever*," he said in 1974, "is *Last Tango in Paris*. That film advanced me twenty years. . . . Because of it I was able to shoot a nude scene in *Thieves Like Us* that I would have been embarrassed to do before and would have covered up."

In the army during World War II, Altman flew numerous B-24 bombing missions over Borneo and the Dutch East Indies. In general, though, he tried to get by "as comfortably as possible." He has said, "I organized an officers' club so I could get to the liquor easiest. My attitude was pretty much like that of Elliott Gould and Donald Sutherland in *M*A*S*H*."

Having written letters and short stories during the war, Altman came home with the idea of becoming a writer. He tried to sell magazine stories, radio shows, and film scripts with little success. He then spent a year in New York City writing, though he actually earned his living by tattooing license numbers on dogs.

When Altman returned to Kansas City, he got a job with the Calvin Company, which made documentary training and sales films for corporations like Gulf Oil and Caterpillar Tractors. There he spent the next eight years becoming a professional filmmaker. "It was a great training period. I wrote, directed, produced, and edited. There wasn't anything I wasn't into." He also had the freedom to do the technical experiments that have always interested him. For one film, for instance, he recorded all the dialogue in a car.

Twice during the 1950s Altman left Kansas City and tried to make it in Hollywood. Both times he had to retreat home "stone broke." Then in 1955 a man he knew asked him to make a film about juvenile delinquents. He wrote, produced, and directed a feature called *The Delinquents*, which was sold to United Artists and got mediocre reviews. Altman himself now owns most of the prints and won't show the film to anyone.

Having left his job for good, Altman, with a partner, made a documentary called *The James Dean Story* for Warner Brothers. It was based on photographs, film clips, reenactments, and interviews with the star's relatives and friends. "I started with the idea of taking Dean to bits," Altman said, "but in the end I guess we all got caught up in the mystique of the man." Altman's later attempts to debunk myths would be more successful.

The film did not do well, but Alfred Hitchcock noticed it and hired Altman to direct some of his half-hour TV mystery shows. Altman directed two, but complained to the producer that the third was "awful." As it turned out, this was a script she personally had developed. "Which left me one way to go," Altman said. "Out."

On the basis of the two Hitchcock credits, and in spite of a reputation for being difficult, Altman was able to build a successful career as a television director. He was the writer, director, and/or producer of more than three hundred hours of television programs. Although he didn't like or respect the work, he says that television taught him useful skills, such as how to shoot fast and cheap. Many of his films have cost less than $2 million, which is very low for Hollywood.

Within limits, Altman filmed TV shows in his own unorthodox style, often losing his job for doing so. One series he worked on was called "Combat." Because the star could never die, Altman would establish another actor as an important character, use him three or four times, and then kill him off. He was finally fired for an antiwar episode he shot without a script. "Kids watch this show," he was told, "and there's not enough jokes for them."

In 1963, at a time when he was making $125,000 a year and had his pick of anything on television, Robert Altman quit. "I finally got tired of the compromise involved in television. . . . By the nature of the medium, it can't be art. What you're doing, you're not doing directly to the audience. There is an intermediary in there, whether it's the agency, or the network, or the sponsors."

During the next few years he got deeper and deeper into debt. He had always spent more than he earned, and there was also the gambling. Then in 1966 he was hired by Warner Brothers to direct *Countdown*, a film about a flight to the moon. Shooting was almost over when Jack Warner saw part of the film in which Altman had two actors talking at the same time. He fired Altman in a fury, cut the film, and added some scenes at the end. The result, according to the *New York Times* critic who saw it, "makes the moon seem just as dull as Mother Earth."

Altman struggled for two more years before he got to direct his first major film, *That Cold Day in the Park*. He wrote the script himself, based on a book to which he and a partner had bought the rights. The story of a psychotic thirty-two-year-old virgin who traps a twenty-year-old boy in her apartment, it was a critical and financial disaster. In fact, Ingo Preminger, producer of *M*A*S*H*, claims that if he had seen that film, he would never have hired Altman. As it was, Altman was his fifteenth choice.

M*A*S*H is the story of two irreverent doctors in a Mobile Army Surgical Hospital in Korea. Hawkeye (Donald Sutherland) and Trapper John (Elliott Gould) are serious surgeons—the best—but less than serious military men. When they are called to Japan to operate on a congressman's son, they bring along their golf clubs. Major Margaret Houlihan, whose role Altman expanded from a cameo of nine lines to that of a major character, calls the army her "home" and is the exact opposite. She is the butt of *M*A*S*H*'s ultimate practical joke. She earns the nickname Hot Lips when her passionate lovemaking with a Bible-toting officer is broadcast over the camp's public address system. Behind the antiwar and counterculture humor, however, is the ever-present gore of the battlefield operating room.

The film was a shocking success. Altman attributes it to timing. Protest against the war in Vietnam was at a high. *M*A*S*H* was chosen as the best film at the Cannes Film Festival and grossed about $40 million, and Altman was nominated for an Academy Award.

Altman earned only a flat fee of $75,000, but *M*A*S*H* got him out of debt and, more important, gave him the means to ensure his independence. In 1963 Altman had founded his own production company and had begun to develop movie projects. After *M*A*S*H*, this production company became Lion's Gate Films, which over the next ten years grew into a ministudio. There, Altman could handle everything from script conferences to film editing. He needed the studios only for financing and distribution. Lion's Gate stayed afloat until 1981, but it was not a profit-making venture. Altman kept plowing the money he earned from his films back into the company.

At the peak of his commercial success, Robert Altman, typically, refused to give Hollywood what it wanted—another *M*A*S*H*. "I always try to push each film a little farther," he explained, "to do things that are a little more difficult for me, to see how far I can make them work."

After making a war film that deglamourized war, Altman played with other traditional movie genres in many of his later films: the caper (*Brewster McCloud*), the psychological thriller (*Images*), the Western (*McCabe and Mrs. Miller* and *Buffalo Bill and the Indians*), the buddy picture (*California Split*), the detective film (*The Long Goodbye*), the period gangster film (*Thieves Like Us*), the musical (*Nashville*), the romantic comedy (*A Wedding* and *A Perfect Couple*), and the science fiction film (*Quintet*). The reason he gave for doing this: "It's telling the audience the medium you are using and, at the same time, reminding them that it *is* only a film."

The films themselves explore themes that interest Altman: what he has called "the flexible boundary between sanity and insanity," and American life today, often as seen through its myths and rituals. Most of the films deal with outsiders, he has said, "people who don't belong there and are trying to cope. I like to tell stories about an alien wandering into a strange place."

Of his next fifteen films, only *Nashville* earned him the great commercial success and critical acclaim that *M*A*S*H* seemed to assure him. *Nashville* followed twenty-four characters through five days on the country music scene. It also drew the comparison between politicians and musical performers. A thin thread of plot holds these elements together. The campaign manager for a third-party candidate is trying to recruit performers for a huge rally. He is ambitious and hypocritical, but so are they.

Altman's characters, who often are not on the screen for long, all suggest great depth. Sometimes it is done with a small detail, like the unmatching wig of Haven Hamilton, the country and western king, or the offhand remark made by the rock couple that they are registered Democrats because her father is.

Altman encouraged his actors to create biographies for their characters and to research their parts. Gwen Welles, who played Sueleen Gay, a waitress and pathetically untalented singer, worked for a while in an airport restaurant before acting in the movie. He is also very perceptive in casting. Keith Carradine, who played Tom, the cool, promiscuous rock singer, said, "Once he hires you for a part, that's it. It means you're right for it and you can't do anything wrong." The casting choice in *Nashville* for which Altman has received most admiration is his decision to give Lily Tomlin the role of Linnea Reese, the gospel singer and mother of two deaf children with whom she communicates in sign language.

Although there were some dissenters, *Nashville* won awards for best director, best film, and best supporting actress (Lily Tomlin) from the New York Film Critics Circle and received five Oscar nominations.

Most of Altman's other films broke even at the box office, but not much more, and met with mixed reviews. Some, like *The*

Long Goodbye (based on a Raymond Chandler story), were marketed wrong by studio executives who missed their satirical intent. But others, like *McCabe and Mrs. Miller*, are also inherently controversial.

McCabe is the story of a man who builds up a frontier town with the help of a tough madam (Mrs. Miller, played by Julie Christie), then is killed by big businessmen who want to take it over. McCabe looks like a Western hero. Altman cast Warren Beatty for the part to ensure that. He is actually something of a fool. ("If you want to make out you're such a fancy dude," Mrs. Miller chides, "you might wear something besides that cheap jockey club cologne.")

The film evoked very different responses from two prominent critics. Pauline Kael, writing in the *New Yorker*, called it "a beautiful pipedream of a movie—a fleeting, almost diaphanous vision of what frontier life might have been." John Simon, on the other hand, in the *New York Times*, complained that the film was "pretentious," "full of plot elements that are left dangling," and "crawling with audiovisual mannerisms."

The two critics responded in opposite ways to Robert Altman's style and to the result he aims for: a film that "will have the effect of making an audience leave the theater impressed and overwhelmed and yet unable to articulate what it has seen, because the picture will have worked on so many senses at the same time." That style is reflected in how his pictures look, how they sound, how they tell their tales, and how they are made.

Robert Altman's films are filled with visual details. He has used the wider screen provided by Panavision for almost all of his pictures. Even so, they often seem to overflow with people and action.

Altman also uses color in a very deliberate way. He wanted *McCabe and Mrs. Miller*, which takes place in 1902, to have the faded look of an old photograph. He also wanted to suggest the lighting of the time—gas or oil lanterns. He and his cinematographer spent hours and hours testing on location before shooting. They finally decided to manipulate the film negative by techniques called flashing and fogging. *Buffalo Bill and the Indians*, Altman's film about the selling of history ("Truth is whatever gets the loudest applause," Bill says), was also supposed to have an antique look. For this film, Altman removed all the blue in the lab, so that yellows, heavy reds, and blacks were exaggerated.

He wanted the film *Three Women*, based on his dream about two young girls who meet in a California desert community and switch personalities, to have a dreamlike quality. For the scenes in the desert, the negatives were overexposed and printed up to give them a faded look. The interiors were done the opposite way. He picked locales very carefully for colors, and the wardrobes and decorations of the apartments tended toward yellows, pinks, and purples—the colors of the desert.

In *Popeye*, his live-action musical version of the comic strip, he wanted a sense of reality at the beginning, even though the characters are two-dimensional. "We didn't go for diffusion," he said, "or anything to give it a sense of distance or antiquity. . . . I muted the colors, the town. As the film progresses, the colors become more specific, cartoony. The reds come out. The wardrobe changes."

The sound of an Altman film is also distinctive. To those who criticize his overlapping dialogue as "inaudible," he answers that it is intended to "give the audience the sense of the dialogue, the emotional feeling rather than the literal word; that's the way sound is in real life." In order to do this well, he developed a special eight-track sound system called Lion's Gate Sound. It records the voices of the actors on separate tracks which can be balanced later. In *Nashville*, he added sixteen tracks for the music.

Altman also often uses a repeated aural theme in his films, usually to add a note of irony or self-consciousness. The muddled loudspeaker announcements in *M*A*S*H*, the Leonard Cohen ballads in *McCabe and Mrs. Miller*, the blaring political slogans from the van in *Nashville*, are some of them. He leaves room for these during shooting and then plugs them in during the editing or sound-mixing stage. Many of these ideas were not even conceived until after the shooting was over.

Perhaps the most controversial element of Altman's style is his focus on behavior and character rather than plot. This is partly a reaction to his many years in television, where he was dealing with hundreds and hundreds of stories in which everything had to be spelled out. "In most films," he once said, "so much specific information is provided that the audience is allowed to be totally uninvolved. I try to make an audience do as much work as they would do reading a novel."

The loose structure of Altman's films suits well his collaborative style of filmmaking. Over the years he has assembled a team of actors and technical people who work on many of his films. Tommy Thompson, for instance, who was assistant director and associate producer on many of Altman's films, began working with him during his TV days. The actors in his "repertory company" include Michael Murphy, Shelley Duvall, Keith Carradine, and Geraldine Chaplin. The idea, he has said, "is to have people around that you know are really cooperative: you want to know that they are in tune with what you are doing and that they respect what you are doing." This also contributes to the success of his casting. "I use a lot of repeats because when I work with an actor I learn what their range is."

Altman is also known for giving people a chance and encouraging creativity. Shelley Duvall had never acted before she met Altman at a party. He gave her a role in *Brewster McCloud*, the story of a boy who wants to fly and a satire on various American follies. Since then she has appeared in many of his films, perhaps most notably as Olive Oyl in *Popeye*.

Joan Tewkesbury, who had directed and adapted only plays,

walked in off the street as an admirer. Altman immediately made her script girl on *McCabe and Mrs. Miller* and then gave her two scripts to write—*Thieves Like Us* and *Nashville*. *Thieves Like Us* was based on a book, but for *Nashville*, she said, he told her only to have someone die at the end. "Otherwise my only instructions were to go to Nashville and see what I could find out." Altman himself added the political theme when the script was finished.

Altman gives his actors an extraordinary amount of freedom and encouragement to improvise: "I don't look for someone to fill a specific part or role so much as I look for an actor who can tell me what that role is about." Some of this is done in front of the camera, but much is done in rehearsal and rewriting. As an extreme example, Shelley Duvall wrote 80 percent of her dialogue in *Three Women*.

In *Nashville* the actors who played country and western singers were encouraged to write their own songs with the help of a professional. Ronee Blakeley, who played the reigning queen of country music in the film, also wrote the scene in which she broke down before an audience. Altman substituted this rambling monologue about her childhood for the scene he had planned. He has said of actors, "The less I impose myself on them, the better the work gets, constantly."

With the actor John Considine, Altman wrote the script for his film *A Wedding*, a satire that observes forty-two characters on a wedding day. Altman and Considine blocked out the scenes according to a wedding schedule and made an outline of character sketches, but wrote no dialogue. "All the actors took these parts without really knowing much of anything about their characters," Altman said. "The minute we had the picture cast I put [two writers] on the film. . . . All of the actors were free to go to any of us to work on their characters' background stories— . . . I had the actors write out their characters' histories—and by the time we began shooting, each actor had a lot of information to work with. And we did encourage the actors to use as much of themselves and their personalities as they would allow themselves to do."

Keith Carradine—who, besides Tom in *Nashville*, played an innocent cowboy in *McCabe and Mrs. Miller*, and the boyish bank robber in *Thieves Like Us*—describes Altman from the actor's point of view: "He sees things in actors they may not even seen in themselves." Paul Newman, who played Buffalo Bill in *Buffalo Bill and the Indians* and Essex in *Quintet*, said that "the most marvelous thing is that there are no egos on the set. . . . No one has any pride of ownership."

As a result, Altman's actors are usually devoted to him. The whole cast of *Nashville*, for instance, worked at rock-bottom wages just to be in his film.

Screenwriters (except for Joan Tewkesbury) are less fond of Altman, however. In fact, he has rarely used the same one twice. Besides allowing his actors to improvise, Altman does a great deal of rewriting himself, often the morning before shooting. Yet he shows no more reverence for his own scripts than for anyone else's. Susannah York, who starred in *Images*, the story of a schizophrenic woman who kills her husband, came up with a better ending than his. Altman immediately struck two sets that were already built in order to use it.

Altman has referred to the screenplay as "a selling tool" for getting financing and after that, "not much more than a production schedule." He said, "I don't consider the dialogue, in most cases, part of the writing. I consider that part of the acting. . . . To me, the writing—the authorship—is in the concept of the film."

Altman himself is responsible for developing the concept and for conveying it to the actors. He does this, in part, by talking to them about their roles, the other characters, and the whole film. He also sets up "the stimuli which the actors will respond to." For *McCabe and Mrs. Miller*, a real town was built on top of a mountain in Canada, building by building, as each new character entered. The actors picked out houses to live in and had square dances at night in the saloon. For *California Split*, Altman hired Amarillo Slim, the champion poker player, to play himself. His contribution to the film, the director said, "was not so much what the audience sees as it was an environment to the people who were there."

Altman always tries to shoot in sequence and to keep the cast together for the full shooting. The result is a close-knit group that meets after work to watch the film from each day's shooting. Carol Burnett said of her experience on the set of A *Wedding*, "It was like summer camp. We all had our kids with us and we had a hoot." A chef is often part of Altman's entourage, and the director admits drinking a Scotch—or two—after hours. ("I don't drink while I'm working," Altman has said. "But I work a lot while I'm drinking.") He is known, however, as a workaholic.

Family life would seem to be a likely victim of this robust man of large appetites, which include a fondness for women, but his wife Kathryn (his third), a witty and elegant woman, seems to be able to cope with him. They have been married for twenty-one years and have two sons. (He also has three children from his previous marriages.) Altman describes her as "terrific" and has said of their marriage, "We really live quite separate lives, but we live them together." And she has said, "He has driven me crazy but he has never bored me."

Lion's Gate, Altman's production company, began to produce other directors' films in the mid-1970s: Alan Rudolph's *Welcome to L.A.* and *Remember My Name*, Robert Benton's *The Late Show*, and Robert Young's *Rich Kids*. Altman saw this, in part, as a way to keep his technical staff employed, but he also wanted to give other filmmakers "the opportunity to make movies the way they want to make them."

In 1979 Lion's Gate greatly expanded and moved into a much larger complex. Unfortunately this move coincided with a downswing in Altman's career. *Quintet*, a film about people playing a morbid game in a bleak future world, which Altman made when his father was dying, was universally panned. *Health*, the story of forty-seven characters at a health food convention, was delayed two years and then released only timidly. Finally, *Popeye* was a critical disappointment and resulted in lawsuits over its great cost ($20 million).

In 1981 Robert Altman sold Lion's Gate. "Suddenly, no one answered my phone calls," he said. "I had no place to turn." He accepted this as the price for being innovative and looked forward to a period of renewal. "I'm merely taking a sabbatical," he said at the time, "and I'm doing something that I've always wanted to do. . . . I think I've been too isolated. I've denied myself the experience of paying attention to the whole spectrum of art: to working in the theater, in opera, in ballet."

Since then, he has directed two short plays by Frank South in New York, both of which got good reviews. He also did a well-publicized staging of Ed Graczyk's *Come Back to the 5 & Dime Jimmy Dean, Jimmy Dean* with Karen Black, Sandy Dennis, and Cher, which failed on Broadway.

But Altman seems to be easing himself back into film. He videotaped the South plays for cable TV. He also shot *Jimmy Dean* in 16-millimeter to be blown up to 35-millimeter for release to art theaters. The film got much better reviews than the play.

For the future, after directing an opera, he plans a film version of another play. "I left the major studios," he said recently. "I didn't leave the movies."

Mel Brooks as the star of *High Anxiety*. PHOTO: Courtesy of 20th Century-Fox

Mel Brooks

The Critic (1963)
The Producers (1967)
The Twelve Chairs (1970)
Blazing Saddles (1974)
Young Frankenstein (1974)
Silent Movie (1976)
High Anxiety (1977)
History of the World—Part I (1981)

"AS LONG AS I AM on the soapbox, farts will be heard," proclaimed Mel Brooks in a flash of the sort of humor that some find hilarious and others find vulgar. And Brooks has been on the soapbox a long time. "As early as I can remember," he said, "I was expected to perform."

Melvin Kaminsky was born on the kitchen table of a tenement in Williamsburg, a predominantly Jewish section of Brooklyn, on June 28, 1926. He never got to know his father, who died when he was two and a half. Some critics and friends see his intense need for approval and fear of death as stemming in part from this loss, which he still mourns. Gene Wilder once described his mental image of Brooks: "I see him standing bare-chested on the top of a mountain, shouting 'Look at me!' and 'Don't let me die!'"

Brooks grew up during the depression. For many years his mother worked long hours in the garment district and then brought more work home at night. But when Melvin was born, his three older brothers were all working so that she could stay home with her beautiful blue-eyed baby. Brooks remembers a delightfully happy childhood, reveling in the adoration of his family. "I was always being tossed in the air, kissed, adored, and pinched." His mother, he said, "had this exuberant joy of living, and she infected me with that. . . . She really was responsible for the growth of my imagination."

His peers were less adoring. They saw him as a little, funny-looking kid who didn't smoke. "But I could talk better than any of them," Brooks said. "I wormed my way in with jokes." If the ebullient side of his humor was born in the family circle, the more caustic side grew up in the outside world. "It comes from not being kissed by a girl until you're sixteen. It comes from feeling that, as a Jew and as a person, you don't fit into the mainstream of American society."

For two years when Melvin was in high school, the Kaminskys lived next door to Buddy Rich, the famous drummer, who gave Mel occasional lessons. When he was fourteen Mel began working during the summers in resort hotels in the Catskill Mountains, the training ground for many great Jewish comedians. He did menial work for room and board and eight dollars a week, and in his free time was allowed to play pool *tummler* (part social director, part buffoon). His main gag was to walk out on the diving board with a suitcase in each hand, announce, "Business is terrible; I can't go on," and jump in.

The summer he was sixteen he was hired as a drummer and part-time *tummler* at one of these hotels. It was then that he changed his name (Brooks is based on Brookman, his mother's maiden name). He didn't want to be confused with the jazz trumpeter Max Kaminsky. That summer two pivotal events occurred: the house comic got sick and Brooks finished the season for him, and he met a saxophone player from a nearby hotel named Sid Caesar.

But Brooks didn't get a chance to develop his taste for performing. World War II was going on, and a month after he graduated from high school, he enlisted in the army. His job was to deactivate land mines ahead of the infantry, but he remembers an unrelated highlight of his wartime service. After the Battle of the Bulge, the Germans made a propaganda pitch to the soldiers over a loudspeaker. Brooks answered with an imitation of Al Jolson singing "Toot Toot Tootsie."

For several months after the war he did shows for enlisted men and officers' clubs. Then he became director, actor, and stagehand in a third-rate summer stock company in New Jersey. When it folded for lack of funds, he went back to the Catskills as a house comic.

In 1947, his acquaintance Sid Caesar asked him to help prepare a revue for television. His first contribution was "Nonentities in the News." Their collaboration lasted almost ten years, through "Your Show of Shows" (with Imogene Coca and Carl Reiner), "Caesar's Hour," and a number of specials. Brooks started out at a weekly salary of $50 and peaked at $5,000.

Caesar's team of writers worked together in endless high-pitched jam sessions. Brooks would jump on furniture and bang his head against the wall. "I had an audience of experts and they showed me no mercy. . . . I was immensely ambitious. It was like I was screaming at the universe to pay attention. Like I had to make *God* laugh."

For Caesar, Brooks created the interview as a new form of comic art. His first invented character was a jungle boy who was brought to New York and put on display. The interviewer asked him, "What in this big city do you fear most, Jungle Boy?" "Buick," Caesar answered. "Buick stronger than lion. Must wait for eyes to go dark before attacking it. When Buick sleep, I sneak up and punch in grill. Buick die."

These years were disastrous for Brooks psychologically. He was depressed and had acute anxiety attacks. "There were fourteen or fifteen occasions when I seriously thought of killing myself," he said. Between 1951 and 1957 he saw a psychoanalyst two to four times a week.

In 1959 his seven-year marriage to a Broadway dancer broke up, separating him from the four children he adores. His problems, he has said, were connected "with accepting life as an adult in the real world. . . . It meant no longer being the baby, the adorable one. It meant being a father figure." He has stayed very close to his daughter and three sons, whom he describes as "these nice friends I've grown."

When "Caesar's Hour" went off the air in 1958, Brooks was again thrown off balance emotionally as well as financially. He tried a variety of projects: he worked on two short-lived Broadway musicals; he wrote a screenplay ("Marriage Is a Dirty Rotten Fraud"), which he couldn't sell; he contributed sketches to a number of TV variety shows; and he began talking about writing a novel to be called *Springtime for Hitler*.

Yet while other Caesar veterans seemed to be prospering, Brooks's career languished. Then one night he and Carl Reiner went into an ad-lib routine they had been doing at parties for years. Reiner would assign Brooks a character—it might be a pirate or a deaf songwriter—and ask him questions. This night he was the 2,000-Year-Old Man. (Asked by Reiner about his children, Brooks answered in a Yiddish accent, "Forty-two thousand children—and not one comes to visit.")

Steve Allen heard the routine and encouraged Brooks and Reiner to make it into a record. The record came out in 1961, and in four years it and several offshoots had sold more than 10 million copies. Brooks said of his character, "The 2,000-Year-Old Man is a pastiche of everyone around me, my mother, my Uncle Joe, my grandmother. When I became him, I could hear 5,000 years of Jews pouring through me."

With this success, Brooks's personality began to mellow. He became less the wild man of his Sid Caesar days. In 1961, he met and fell in love with the actress Anne Bancroft. After a courtship of three years, they were married, and they now have an eleven-year-old son.

If the pair seems incongruous ("Beauty and the Beast," some friends call them), it is only on the surface. Carl Reiner explains their devotion to each other this way: "They both are sharp and bright and volatile—quick to anger, quick to forgive." Besides, Brooks's private self is different from his public self. "When he's being himself," said the novelist Joseph Heller, a longtime friend, "he'll talk quietly for hours and then make a remark that's unforgettably funny because it came out of a real situation." He is warm and loving, deeply loyal to his friends, and generous to needy members of his family.

During the 1960s, Brooks had another success—the television series "Get Smart," which he created with another writer. This was a James Bond spoof, with an idiotic secret agent hero (Maxwell Smart), who was constantly locking himself in closets and tripping over his own feet. Smart worked for CONTROL, a secret agency of the United States. His enemy was the international agency KAOS. The show was a hit from its first episode (in which the character Mr. Big was played by a dwarf). But it was often criticized for bad taste.

Later, in 1967, when "Get Smart" was well established, Brooks was offered a series of his own, but he turned it down. "TV grinds you up, makes a sausage out of you every week," he said. He ventured back to television only once again, about ten years later, as executive producer and script supervisor for a satirical version of the Robin Hood legend called "When Things Were Rotten." He explained at the time that he "couldn't resist the fun of [a tax collector] saying, 'Hold your tongue,' and [all the peasants] holding their tongues." The show got good reviews at first, but the joke was too limited to be sustained for long.

Mel Brooks got his first taste of moviemaking in 1963, when he conceived, wrote, and narrated *The Critic*. This three-minute film was a satire of the arty, abstract geometric cartoons that were popular at the time. The narrator was a simple old Jewish man sitting in the theater. "Dis is cute, dis is cute, dis is nice," he says. "Vat da hell is it? It must be some symbolism. . . . I think it's symbolic of junk." Brooks shared an Academy Award with his cartoonist for best short subject in the cartoon category.

His first feature-length film, *The Producers*, came four years later. It is the story of a down-and-out theatrical producer, Max Bialystock (played by Zero Mostel), and a timid accountant who deliberately put together a dreadful play *(Springtime for Hitler)*. The play includes girls in a swastika formation singing Brooks's song "Here Comes the Master Race" ("Don't be shtoopid, be a schmarty, come and join the Nazi party"). It is supposed to close as soon as it opens, allowing them to pocket all the money invested in it, but instead it is a smash. The two producers and their star go to jail, where they are last seen rehearsing—and overselling shares in—a new musical, *Prisoners of Love*.

This film was Brooks's way of attacking bigotry and expressing his outrage at the Holocaust. "I think you can bring down totalitarian governments faster," he said, "by using ridicule than you can with invective."

Brooks cast Gene Wilder, who had played opposite his wife in a Brecht play, as the accountant Leo Bloom. Wilder was to become the new vehicle for Brooks's humor as well as his closest friend and most vehement fan. He also became the cornerstone of an informal repertory company, which also included Madeline Kahn, Dom DeLuise, Marty Feldman, Cloris Leachman, and Harvey Korman. Brooks uses the same actors over and over, he has said, because he wants "to surround myself with people I love—make a family."

Brooks fought hard to direct *The Producers* himself, less from the desire to be a film director than in "self-defense." He explains:

"Basically, I'm a writer. I'm the proprietor of the vision. I also know what I eventually want to happen on the screen. So if you have a valuable idea, the only way to protect it is to direct it." In fact, Brooks does much more than that. He takes part in all artistic decisions, including what color the title will be. He also stays with his films through release, supervising every detail of the advertising campaign.

His directing experience at that point, however, was limited to the trailer for one movie. But he was a passionate moviegoer, even as a child ("This was my school—the movies," he has said), and has claimed that "simply seeing movies, you pick up a good deal. I always knew what actors should say to one another and how they should look, and I always understood stage business. That is, should they have a pencil in their hands or be brushing their teeth or peering up a drainpipe when they say, 'I love you.'"

But Brooks's inexperience showed. He himself tells the story of his first day on the set when he dramatically yelled, "Cut!" instead of "Roll 'em!" He also admits that he basically set up the camera and let the actors run around in front of the lens. "I had no idea as to how I would capture the vision that was in my mind on film."

In one respect, though, Brooks was very professional in making *The Producers* and has continued to be in all his films. He finished shooting on schedule and spent only $941,000, which was less than the budget.

Although most critics enjoyed the wild humor of *The Producers*, many considered it too vulgar. Renata Adler summed up the reaction in her review in the *New York Times*, calling it a "violently mixed bag. Some of it is shoddy and gross and cruel; the rest is funny in an entirely unexpected way."

The Producers developed a cult following and was in the black in four years. In addition, Brooks won an Academy Award for best original screenplay.

His next film, *The Twelve Chairs*, took three years to make, including a year of shooting in Yugoslavia. He adapted it from a satiric Russian novel of the 1920s which he had loved as a child. (Brooks is a passionate reader.) It follows three men—a con man, an impoverished aristocrat, and a conniving priest—as they search for twelve dining room chairs in which a fortune in jewels was hidden from the Bolsheviks. "It has all the craziness and *meshugas* that I love," Brooks said, "humanity, greed, destruction, happiness—brush strokes of tenderness. It's the kind of pot I like to stew around in a lot." He wrote the theme song himself— "Hope for the Best/Expect the Worst"—and shot a lot of it "on my belly in the fields."

While the set of *The Producers* had been marked by violent outbursts of temper, the set of this film was harmonious, and Brooks won the admiration of his actors. Today, well-known actors who are not Brooks regulars often seek parts in his films for pure fun and for the experience of working with him.

Although *The Twelve Chairs* was a box office failure and was generally panned, critics agreed that Brooks was outstanding as Tikon, the caretaker of a home for the aged who longs for the good old days of servitude. He recalls his old master: "I loved him. He hardly ever beat us."

Brooks has said that this film "taught me something. There is no room in the business now for a special little picture. You either hit 'em over the head or stay home with the canary." His next four films—all genre satires—hit 'em over the head. The first, *Blazing Saddles*, came to him as a script titled "Tex X" by Andrew Bergman. Since he couldn't stir up any interest in his own projects and because he liked the idea of a modern black man, with double knits and Gucci saddlebags, living in the Old West, he agreed to work on it. But this time he didn't work alone. He went back to the jam session style of his Caesar years and shared the writing with Bergman and three other writers.

Blazing Saddles is about a black sheriff named Bart (Cleavon Little) hired to defend a small town against an evil land-grabbing lawyer, who hopes Bart will be lynched by the bigoted townspeople. Gene Wilder plays the sheriff's sidekick, the Waco Kid, a legendary, quick-draw gunman, now an alcoholic. Madeline Kahn plays Lilli von Shtupp, a bar singer who talks like Marlene Dietrich with a speech impediment. She even writes that way. "I must see you wight away," says her note to Bart. "Please come to my dwessing woom." Brooks himself plays two roles—the corrupt, lecherous governor Lepetomain and a Yiddish-speaking Indian chief.

The film is a mixture of satire, parody, farce, and bathroom humor. It ends with a painted cardboard model of the town and its citizens, built as an ambush for the bad guys. Their battle overflows onto a real Hollywood set where a musical is being rehearsed. Finally, Bart and Waco ride into the sunset, only to abandon their horses for a chauffered limousine, Brooks's last laugh at the movie version of the West.

Brooks said of *Blazing Saddles*, "I figured my career was finished anyway, so I wrote berserk, heartfelt stuff about white corruption and racism and Bible-thumping bigotry. We used dirty language on the screen for the first time, and to me the whole thing was like a big psychoanalytic session. I just got everything out of me—all my furor, my frenzy, my insanity, my love of life, and my hatred of death."

He had no idea it would be a box office hit. In fact, at the first screening, for Warners executives, there was hardly a laugh, even at the scene where a chain gang boss tells his prisoners to sing a typical black work song and they break into Cole Porter's "I Get a Kick Out of You." Later that night, in a room filled with all the other Warners employees, there were roars. Thus was born Brooks's tradition of doing his screenings before a large, diverse audience.

The film was accused of being chaotic, but Brooks denies the charge. "It was calculated chaos," he said. "I'm a very well-trained maniac." Brooks has said that he takes two years to make a picture—eighteen months for writing and six for production. "I write and rewrite for the kind of comedy I do, keep pads and pencils all over the house, jotting down new lines and dialogue that comes to mind any time of day or night."

He also claims that every scene and almost every line of his films is in the script. "You can improvise with rhythms and motions during rehearsals," he said, "but not with lines." He has a three-week preparation period before shooting. "I take the crew, and we meet every day and go from page one to page one hundred twenty. Every department raises their hand and says, 'What do we do here?' I'm very organized, so that we know every day exactly what we should accomplish, and what is needed to accomplish it, both artistically and technically. We plan every move, every camera angle. . . ."

While they were finishing *Blazing Saddles*, Gene Wilder came up with the idea for *Young Frankenstein*. He wrote the first draft, and Brooks revised it. 20th Century-Fox gave them $2.8 million and has remained loyal to Brooks ever since. He always has final cut, a guarantee that the studio won't change the film once he is done with it.

Young Frankenstein is the story of the great-grandson of Dr. Beaufort Frankenstein. Young Frederick is a modern brain surgeon who returns to the ancestral estate and is seduced by the idea of creating a man. Wilder played Young Frankenstein and Marty Feldman was the hunchback assistant Igor, whose hump keeps switching sides. Madeline Kahn played Young Frankenstein's frigid fiancée. They rub elbows good-bye so that he won't muss up her makeup, clothes, or hairdo. Her sexuality is finally excited by "old zipper-neck," as she calls the monster. In the film's happy ending, Frankenstein arranges to share some of his intellectual endowment with the monster in exchange for some of the monster's sexual prowess.

Brooks described *Young Frankenstein* as his first attempt at half laughs and half story, resulting in a more straightforward plot. The film was very successful at the box office. It also got better reviews than any Brooks film before, and it received several raves.

He was praised for his camera work and his fastidious attention to detail. Brooks did a lot of research so that everything in the film, right down to the acting, could be done in 1930s style. "We wanted to make a hilarious pastiche of the old black-and-white horror films of the thirties," he said, and "we wanted to offer sincere and reverent homage to those same beautifully made movies." *Young Frankenstein* was shot in black-and-white, and Brooks used techniques of the thirties like sudden closeups and cuts, halos around the heads, and swirling fog around the castle. Half of the scientific machinery came from the sets of old Frankenstein films.

Brooks paid vigilant attention to pacing and nuance. He directs with an eye to editing, always aware of both ends of a joke, and he is very careful. There is a four-minute scene between the monster and a lonely blind man (Gene Hackman), who thinks he has a longed-for visitor. It is filled with slapstick humor, as he pours soup on the monster's lap, smashes his glass in a toast, and lights his thumb instead of a cigar. This scene took four days (from 6:00 A.M. to 9:00 P.M.) to shoot to Brooks's satisfaction.

Brooks also worked very closely with the editor, going through the film frame by frame at least twelve times. The decision as to where and when to cut was usually Brooks's. He has said that editing is like rewriting, and has described the way he works: "My principle of cutting is you start with a scalpel and end with a blunt ax. Everyone usually does it the other way around. You know, knocking out whole scenes and ending by refining. But I start by taking out an 'and,' an 'if,' or a 'but.' I play with a scene. Then when you have the rough cut, you start eliminating scenes."

As a filmmaker, Mel Brooks is of two minds about his art. On the one hand, he has said, "I'm trying to get back to . . . the golden age of comedy with Laurel and Hardy, with Chaplin, with

Buster Keaton, just flat-out smash belly-comedy." On the other hand, he often attributes serious themes to his films, and he has said that he needs a "philosophical base" in his comedy. *The Producers* and *Blazing Saddles* are about bigotry, and he has said that *Young Frankenstein* is about man's dream of being a god and about what he calls "womb envy."

Brooks described his next movie (and next hit)—*Silent Movie*—as an "experimental" film. It was a joint project with a group of writers who stayed together for another film also. In *Silent Movie*, Mel Funn (Brooks), a washed-up, reformed alcoholic Hollywood director, tries to save his studio from takeover by the conglomerate Engulf and Devour by making a silent film. He is assisted by Marty Eggs (Feldman) and Dom Bell (DeLuise).

"It was very difficult for me," he said. "because all my training has been vocal. . . . So I did *Silent Movie* as a kind of punishment, as a task, as an exercise to expand my visual muscles." Although this movie has very noisy sound effects, there is no dialogue except the single word "no," spoken by the mime Marcel Marceau.

Silent Movie gave Brooks his first leading role. When Gene Wilder wasn't available, Brooks himself decided to play the part of Funn. But he worried about it. "One of the requirements of a film," said the stocky comic with rubbery features, "is to deliver nice-looking people to the audience."

With one success as a star and with Wilder still unavailable, Brooks gave himself the leading role in his next film, *High Anxiety*. This Hitchcock spoof is the story of Dr. Richard H. Thorndyke, a psychiatrist with a fear of heights, who is appointed to head the Psycho-Neurotic Institute for the Very, Very Nervous. He must take control away from greedy evildoers. The rate of recovery at the expensive clinic, the assistant director figures out on his pocket calculator, is "once in a blue moon." Unfortunately, the institute is located on top of a hill.

Brooks called the film "an homage to Hitchcock, who has been

Mel Brooks as the director of *High Anxiety*. PHOTO: Courtesy of 20th
Century-Fox

my favorite director since I was five years old." His research included seeing every Hitchcock film at least a dozen times, and he even went to the master for his blessing. Brooks tried to make *High Anxiety* look like a Hitchcock film, and it makes many references to his work, including a scene of birds (pigeons rather than bloodthirsty crows) attacking with mayonnaise and spinach droppings.

He also used a scene from *The Lodger*, which had haunted him since he was a child. In that film the camera shoots a man walking on a glass floor from below; in *High Anxiety* the camera is under a glass coffee table. At a critical moment, a coffee pot is put down, obscuring the view. "The camera gets frantic," he said. "Finally the lens is wiped out with a tray of strudel."

Another target for spoof in the film is psychiatry itself. Thorndyke explains, for instance, that he once considered a singing career, but "the big bucks are in psychiatry. I mean, it's so much more emotionally involving."

Again Brooks worked very carefully, keeping his three cowriters on the set as continual advisers, scrutinizing video replays of each take with the actors.

Some critics called the film uneven and vulgar, but Brooks's audience paid more than $20 million to see it in the first year.

His most recent film, *History of the World—Part I*, is made up of six historical sketches. Brooks was producer, director, writer, and star. He played Louis XVI; a dancing, singing Torquemada; and Comicus, a stand-up philosopher who is out of work and settles for a job as a waiter. (At the Last Supper, he asks, "Are you all together or is it separate checks?")

Although many of the criticisms were the same as always, Vincent Canby in the *New York Times* wrote that, in his opinion, this film "redefines and clarifies" the comic methods of the others. "The point of Mr. Brooks's use of foul language, obscene gestures, a preoccupation with bodily functions and with sex as the single most overwhelmingly human impulse is to remind us that we may not be quite as civilized as is otherwise indicated."

In the immediate future, a sequel to *History of the World* seems inevitable. The film even ends with "Coming Attractions" (including "Jews in Space"). It is also likely that, having laid out his territory of wild, low comedy, Brooks will not abandon it or his huge audience. "It's one of the great joys of my life," he has said, "to walk down the aisle toward the screen, spin around and slowly walk back up while the audience is laughing at my work."

Francis Coppola

Francis Coppola

THE CAREER OF FRANCIS COPPOLA heads in two different directions at once. Part of him aims to be a serious film artist, the other part wants to be a rich and powerful movie mogul. Because of his ambition to combine the two (and perhaps also because of his ample waistline and bushy beard), he has been compared with Orson Welles.

Coppola's instinct for showmanship did not really surface until college. He was born on April 7, 1939, in Detroit, the second of three children of Italia and Carmine Coppola. He has described himself as a child as "funny-looking, not good in school, near-sighted," an unpopular kid "immersed in a fantasy world." He was nicknamed "Science" at school because he was always tinkering with gadgets.

51

His younger sister is the actress Talia Shire, who played Connie Corleone in *The Godfather* (and was actually hired for the film before Francis was). His older brother August is a writer and college English professor, who ran an educational and apprenticeship program for Francis's Zoetrope Studios. Francis grew up viewing August as "handsomer, brilliant, the adored one of any group."

Although the Coppolas lived a suburban middle-class life, it was not an entirely sunny one. The family moved about thirty times as Carmine, a flutist, conductor, and composer, searched for conducting jobs. "Our lives centered on what we all felt was the tragedy of his career," according to Francis. "He was a very talented man . . . he felt that his own music never really emerged." As soon as he had the power, Coppola hired his father to work on his productions—from college plays to his first films. Finally, Carmine Coppola won an Oscar, shared with the famous composer Nino Rota, for the score of *The Godfather— Part II*. "That moment was so great," his son has said, "I really didn't care whether I got an Oscar or not."

At the age of nine, Francis Coppola began his theatrical career. He had developed polio (like Harry Caul in *The Conversation*) and was confined to bed for a year. For company he had a 16-millimeter movie projector, a tape recorder, a record player, a television set, a ventriloquist's dummy, and comic books. ("They're just like screenplays.") He put on puppet shows regularly and created sound tracks for the silent movies he showed on his bedroom wall.

When he was fourteen, he made his first film by cutting up the family's home movies to recast himself as the hero. He edited them into features with titles like *The Rich Millionaire* and *The Lost Wallet*. At a military high school he attended briefly, Coppola wrote the book and lyrics for the class musical. He also wrote love letters for fellow cadets, charging them a dollar a page.

He graduated from high school in Great Neck, a suburb of

New York where his parents finally settled, and went on to Hofstra University on Long Island, on a drama scholarship. After seeing Sergei Eisenstein's *Ten Days That Shook the World*, he had decided to become a filmmaker. But he wanted to model his career after that of the Russian director and study theater first.

At Hofstra, Coppola was a big man on campus. He wrote for and edited the student literary magazine; he directed plays, including a musical, which he staged with a thirty-piece professional orchestra; and he wrote the book and lyrics for an original musical comedy. He won three awards for theatrical direction and production. He also took a stab at filmmaking. In his junior year he sold his car to buy a 16-millimeter camera. But he didn't finish the movie he tried to make because, he said, "I just didn't have the technical expertise."

Perhaps Coppola's greatest accomplishment, however, and the signpost for the future was managing to merge the school's drama group and musical comedy club, thus gaining control of a $30,000 yearly budget.

After he graduated in 1959, Coppola went, as planned, to film school at UCLA. But he found it disappointing. The students were all pessimistic about ever being able to succeed in Hollywood without compromising their art. While they sat around bemoaning their fate, Coppola was making movies. For small fees, he directed some "very innocent" sex films with titles like *The Peeper, Tonight for Sure*, and *The Belt Girls and the Playboy*.

It was through these that he got his education: "You do everything yourself, from first script to final editing. . . . You learn the fullest use to which each element in moviemaking can be put . . . and you learn how to make the most out of every dollar in the budget."

He also became an assistant to Roger Corman, king of the low-budget horror film. His first assignment, though he knew no Russian, was to write an English script for a Russian science fiction film and turn it into a monster movie. He worked on four more Corman films as sound man, dialogue director, and associate producer, and then was rewarded with a horror picture of his own.

In three and a half days Coppola wrote the script for *Dementia 13*, the story of a doomed family, which includes the required number of ax murders. Corman gave him $20,000 and a cast and crew already on location in Ireland. (The art director of *Dementia 13* was Eleanor Neil, a graphic artist who is now Coppola's wife and the mother of his three children.) Coppola, typically, managed to obtain another $20,000 for his film by selling British rights. *Dementia 13* got some kind reviews but many negative ones.

Coppola won first prize in the Samuel Goldwyn writing competition in 1962 for a screenplay titled *Pilma, Pilma*. Although it has never been produced, it gave him an entrée to Hollywood—as a staff writer for Seven Arts, a company that put together films for major studios. He wrote ten or twelve screenplays in two years, but the few that reached the screen bore little resemblance to what he had written. And still he couldn't persuade anyone to let him direct. "In fact," he has said, "I wrote a screenplay about a guy who wants to direct a movie so bad he goes crazy, just to put my position more strongly across."

Coppola took his first big gamble with $20,000 he had saved from his salary. He invested it all in the stock market, hoping to turn it into enough money to make a movie. Instead, he lost his entire investment.

Meanwhile his reputation as a writer was growing, and 20th Century-Fox hired him to write a screenplay about World War II General George Patton. His script, which portrayed the general as "a man out of his time, a pathetic hero, a Don Quixote figure," was scrapped by the studio. But later George C. Scott, who eventually starred in the movie, resurrected it, and in 1970 Francis Coppola won his first Oscar as coauthor of the screenplay for *Patton*.

While he was still working for Seven Arts by day, Coppola had spent his nights writing a screenplay based on an English novel titled *You're a Big Boy Now*, for which he owned the rights. He sold the rights to Seven Arts and was finally hired as a director. The film is a farce about an adolescent boy who takes a job in the New York Public Library and tries to overcome his shyness and fear of girls. It was one of the first films to use rock music for its score.

With his charm and audacity, Coppola managed to persuade New York Mayor John V. Lindsay to allow him to film the star (Peter Kastner) roller-skating through the stacks of the solemn library. He also persuaded three prominent stars who had never heard of him before—Rip Torn, Geraldine Page, and Julie Harris—to appear in the film.

Although many reviewers found the humor in the film too absurd, his talent—especially his sensitive use of actors—was generally acknowledged. The film, whose budget grew from $250,000 to $1 million, lost money, but it accomplished two purposes for Coppola: it earned him his master's degree from UCLA and, more important, it drew attention to him as a director.

Coppola was already fascinated by the new technology available to filmmakers. He made a videotape of the actors performing a separate rehearsal script he wrote for *Big Boy*, which he then studied. This gave the actors a chance to develop their parts and the director a sense of what his picture was going to be like before he even began shooting.

The next picture Coppola took on—*Finian's Rainbow*, a Hollywood musical based on the 1940s Broadway show—brought accusations that he was selling out. The film is about a leprechaun with a crock of gold that grants wishes and is used to turn a white senator black. Coppola had decided to write his own screenplay based on the original book rather than use a topical adapation. Unfortunately, he wasn't done writing when shooting had to begin, and the material was too dated anyway. Other problems beyond his control, including a miscast leprechaun and a bad choreographer, helped to make the film a gigantic flop.

Before the extent of this fiasco was apparent, Warner Brothers offered Coppola $400,000 to direct *Mame*, another musical. But he turned it down in order to make *The Rain People*, a personal film based on a story he had written in college. With the money he had earned from *Finian*, he bought a van and $80,000 worth of equipment, including a complex editing machine that gave him the ability to edit as he went along.

Then he got Warner Brothers to invest in the film, which is about a pregnant woman who leaves her husband and her responsibilities one rainy morning and drives west, befriending a brain-damaged football player on the way. According to Coppola, it "rests on the idea of human responsibility—what we owe each other, what we owe ourselves."

A seventeen-member crew in seven vehicles made that pilgrimage with the main character for four months across eighteen states. Before they left, Coppola rehearsed the cast for three weeks with a special script written for the stage.

Although Coppola was writing as they went along and would incorporate interesting things they saw, the style of the film, he has said, "was not that of improvisation. But we hoped to get the flavor of improvisation. The basis was scripted, thought out—and, hopefully, is thematically whole."

The film was a financial failure, and the reviews were generally lukewarm, criticizing the plot, the pace, and the inconclusive ending, but usually praising the actors' performances.

In 1969, before *The Rain People* was released, Coppola had already organized from the crew of that film the core of what was to be his own company. American Zoetrope was named after a nineteenth-century device, a revolving drum with slits in it, which created the first motion picture. Thus really began the second branch of his career—as a movie mogul.

American Zoetrope was located on three floors of a converted warehouse in downtown San Francisco. It had editing rooms, screening rooms, and the newest, most advanced equipment—everything needed to make movies except a sound stage. There were twelve to fifteen staff members and eight filmmakers. "What we're really doing," Coppola said at the time, "is giving these young filmmakers a chance to make films." But the company was also, he said, "a true capitalist venture, designed to sustain itself and provide artistic freedom through money." He got Warner Brothers to invest $3.5 million.

Unfortunately, after six months Warners didn't like what it saw and withdrew its money, leaving Coppola with his equipment and his facility and half a million dollars in debt. When Paramount asked him to direct and coauthor the screenplay for the movie version of the best-selling novel *The Godfather*, it was, as the line in the movie goes, "an offer he couldn't refuse."

This is the story of a Mafia family, the Corleones, from the end of World War II to the mid-1950s, when the power passes from father to son. Originally slated as a conventional gangster movie, the three-hour epic grossed about $300 million worldwide and won three Academy Awards—for best picture, best actor, and best screenplay based on another medium. Jay Cocks, the *Time* magazine critic, wrote of *The Godfather*: "In its blending of new depth with an old genre, it becomes that rarity, a mass entertainment that is also great movie art."

Cocks also wrote that "no American film before *The Godfather* has caught so truly the texture of an ethnic subculture." Coppola drew from his memories of family rituals authentic and colorful details for the wedding at the beginning of the film and the christening at the end. Even so simple a detail as a man entering his mother's kitchen and, before anything else, dipping a piece of bread in the pot simmering on the stove rings true of Italian-American life.

The major criticism of the film was that it romanticized the Mafia, that criminals were portrayed as adventurers. But Coppola said in answer, "I felt it was making a harsh statement about the Mafia and power at the end of *Godfather I* when Michael [the new Godfather] murders all those people, then lies to his wife and closes the door." He also said that the Mafia is a metaphor for America. The first line of the film, he pointed out, is "I believe in America."

The violence in this world is made explicit. People are shot, strangled, and blown up in cars. In one particularly gruesome episode, a movie company executive who was not cooperating with the mob finds the bloody head of his prize horse on his bed.

The filming itself was not all easy sailing. As the budget soared from $1 million to over $5 million, the studio began to get worried and, according to Coppola, "I was getting 'fired' every other week. The things they were going to fire me over were . . . wanting to cast Brando [as Don Vito, the Godfather], wanting to cast Pacino [as Michael], wanting to shoot in Sicily, wanting to make it in period. The very things that made the film different from any other film."

The crew members and actors also feared that the young director didn't know what he was doing. Coppola always shoots scenes over and over until he gets an actor's best performance. As a result, his rough cuts (before editing) always look dreadful. "What you select in editing is part of the writing process," he has said. "It was in the post-production for Part I that I found what we had—those performances from Brando and Pacino that knit the film together."

In fact, it was the actors' performances that again brought Coppola the greatest praise. He used one unusual technique before shooting began. He gave a dinner for the cast at which he asked them to improvise. They naturally began to act like a family, all competing for Brando's attention. On the set, though, he has said, "I may sometimes get my actors to improvise, but it is always within a framework and to make a point that I have decided on. After all, I am the only one who can know how the whole film is going to shape and precisely what the function of any particular piece will be."

Between *The Godfather* and the inevitable sequel, Coppola directed a play and an opera in San Francisco. He said that he needed to do something different, "something where I could experiment more freely, without political or financial pressures."

During that time, he also wrote the screenplay for *The Great Gatsby*, directed by Jack Clayton, which generally got poor reviews. Before this, Coppola had thought of himself mainly as a writer and of writing as "the primary act of creation." Afterwards, however, he said, "I was so impressed by how badly *Gatsby* worked that I started to put more credit to what a director does."

After *The Godfather*, Paramount formed the jointly owned Directors Company, with Coppola, Peter Bogdanovich, and William Friedkin, the three major directors of the day. The studio had agreed to finance and distribute their films, but the deal fell through after only three were made. One of these was *The Conversation*, which Coppola wrote and directed. He chose this personal film, costing less than $2 million, he said, because "at that point in my career the most important thing was to confirm to myself that I could do original work."

The Conversation is a psychological thriller about a professional wiretapper, Harry Caul ("the best bugger on the West Coast"). Although he is compulsively private himself (his own girl friend doesn't know what he does or how to reach him), he becomes emotionally involved in an assignment. He overhears a sentence, "He'd kill us if he got the chance," on a tape he was hired to make and is convinced that an attractive young couple are going to be murdered. Haunted by another assignment that led to deaths, he tries to withhold the tapes. "I wasn't making a film about *privacy*, as I had set out to do," Coppola said, "but rather, once again, a film about *responsibility*, as was *The Rain People*."

He used the camera and the sound track to give the audience

the sense of eavesdropping on Harry's personal life. The very static camera "gave the impression that it didn't have an operator on it," he said, "so that the actor would walk out of the frame, just as if it were an electronic camera." He also tried to make the sound track from Harry's point of view: "I wrote many scenes to be sound-oriented like a murder occurring in another room that you don't see but you hear."

The film was very well received by critics. Stephen Farber in the *New York Times* called it "Coppola's best movie, a landmark film of the seventies, and a stunning piece of original American fiction. It also won the highest award at the Cannes Film Festival. But it was not popular at the box office.

While he was still editing *The Conversation*, Coppola was frantically writing and shooting *The Godfather—Part II*. To the reporters who kept asking him why he agreed to do this sequel, Coppola gave a number of answers. Among them were the challenge this time of being allowed to do whatever he wanted and the desire to make a statement about power by linking Michael Corleone directly to big business and corrupt politicians. "And to be completely honest," he told one reporter, "there was the possibility of my making so much money I could bankroll some of my other projects."

That is exactly what happened. Coppola reportedly got 15 percent of the film's gross profits. In addition, though, *The Godfather—Part II* is considered by many critics to be the most significant American film of the decade. It won six Oscars, including those for best picture, best director, best screenplay, and best original dramatic score.

The film, which is twenty-five minutes longer than *The Godfather*, juxtaposes the fall of Michael, the new Godfather, with flashbacks of his father's rise a half-century earlier. Young Vito is seen at the turn of the century fleeing Sicily, where his parents and older brother were killed. In New York, Vito (played by Robert De Niro) avenges their deaths and rises to power in the neighborhood, partly by protecting the weak. Meanwhile, Michael's main concern is gaining greater control of Las Vegas gambling. He becomes a less and less attractive figure and by the end of the film is all alone, betrayed by his brother and abandoned by his wife.

Ironically, the film's structure, which has been especially praised, was a last-minute decision made just weeks before it was released. For a long time Coppola worried that he had two different films, shot in different styles, with "a different smell to them." He crowded friends and associates into the editing rooms, using their reactions to help sort this out.

In 1975, Francis Coppola's personal fortune included a legitimate theater, a radio station, and large real-estate holdings. To this he added a large investment in a film distribution company and in *City*, a San Francisco–based magazine, which he attempted unsuccessfully to publish and edit. *City* folded in early 1976, just as Coppola left for the Philippines to begin filming *Apocalypse Now*.

This film about the Vietnam War uses as its framework Joseph Conrad's novel *Heart of Darkness*. An army captain named Willard (Martin Sheen) is assigned to "terminate with extreme prejudice" the command of Colonel Kurtz (Marlon Brando), who has gone mad and become emperor of a band of Cambodian natives deep in the jungle. Willard's long boat ride up the river to this quarry highlights many of the horrors of war. In one bizarre scene, a lieutenant orders a village strafed to clear the water for a famous surfer traveling with Willard.

Coppola spent almost four years and $30 million making this controversial film. The emotional strain nearly cost him his marriage. And because no studio would support the project financially, he had to do it himself. The filming was plagued by discomfort and misfortune. There was unbearable heat and persistent rain. The cast and crew suffered from dysentery. A typhoon destroyed $1 million worth of sets, and Martin Sheen had a heart attack three-quarters of the way through filming. "There were times," Coppola said later, "when I thought I was going to die, literally, from the inability to move the problems I had."

The original script for the film was written by John Milius almost ten years earlier as one of the American Zoetrope projects Warner Brothers turned its back on. But it was not what Coppola wanted—it didn't have enough of the Conrad novel in it—so he decided to rewrite it himself. He had a list of two hundred points he wanted to make about the war, including the fact that the use of drugs was widespread, that many of the soldiers were naive seventeen-year-olds, that most of them were black, and that the top officers were living extravagantly.

Early in the morning, he would sit in his houseboat writing the script on index cards. At night he would review videocassettes of the film. When Marlon Brandon arrived to play Kurtz, his part wasn't ready. He and Coppola together worked out various versions of his important monologue and taped them.

Coppola shot a million feet of film during the sixteen months of filming and then spent two years trying to shape it. He boldly previewed the film in Los Angeles in 1979, passing out a sealed questionnaire that was "my invitation to you to help me finish the film." He also entered it in the Cannes Film Festival as "work in progress" because he still hadn't settled on an ending. That gamble paid off. The film shared the grand prize.

Coppola said of *Apocalypse Now*, "I tried to make it more of an experience than a movie." He used no documentary footage: "Every shot in that film was shot on a long dolly and was very operatic and lyrical. I used red and orange smoke right from the beginning to tell you it was all an opera."

The film got generally good reviews, and his rendering of the war in the first two-thirds was praised. But many critics found the meeting between Willard and Kurtz, who quotes T. S. Eliot, "pretentious" and not worthy of comparison with Conrad.

By 1981, when the film broke even, Coppola had already

expanded his empire. The year before, he had bought the Hollywood General Studio, built in 1919, for $6.7 million. He now had ten acres in the heart of Hollywood and a facility with nine sound stages, projection rooms, thirty-four editing rooms, and a special effects shop. Zoetrope Studios was born. Here he planned to create an updated version of the studio system of the 1930s— actors and writers under contract, senior filmmakers on tap, "a family of people working together from inception to final product." He also planned to develop what he calls electronic cinema, the use of computer and video equipment in filmmaking.

Zoetrope put its stamp on three films: *The Escape Artist*, directed by Caleb Deschanel; *Hammett*, directed by Wim Wenders, but shelved indefinitely; and Coppola's own film *One from the Heart*. The studio also began to distribute films of foreign directors in this country.

But almost immediately there were crises. The budget of *One from the Heart* soared from $15 million to $27 million, and investors pulled out. Coppola was saved only by last-minute loans and a staff willing to work for half-pay. But the film itself did poorly at the box office, leaving him in financial trouble.

One from the Heart is a love story. An ordinary couple—she is a travel agent and he owns a wrecking company—fight and break up on the eve of the anniversary of their meeting. They both go to Las Vegas for the Fourth of July weekend and meet romantic lovers. Hers is a Latin waiter and singer (Raul Julia); his is a circus acrobat (Nastassia Kinski). But they are drawn back together for a happy ending.

At great cost, Coppola recreated Las Vegas on the Zoetrope lot. He wanted to give the film a magical, unreal quality. After the experience of *Apocalypse Now*, he also wanted to be in complete control. And he was. Before shooting even began, he was able to see the whole film. He videotaped artists' sketches of more than five hundred scenes and recorded the actors reading a radio play version of the script. He directed the film from a silver trailer

Coppola on the set of *One from the Heart*.

(dubbed Image Control), which held a computer, TV monitors, microphones, and telephones. He could see exactly what the camera lens was focusing on and could adjust and edit each sequence as it was shot.

Reviews of the film ranged from the lukewarm, questioning whether the love story was strong enough to support the technological splendor of the production, to the harsh. David Ansen wrote in *Newsweek*, "What happens is that the style overwhelms everything. The audience literally applauds the sets but loses sight of the characters."

Nevertheless, Coppola insists that it is "probably the most interesting movie I've ever made." He and his electronic cinema quickly moved on to Tulsa, where he began shooting two films based on teenage novels by S. E. Hinton—*The Outsiders* and *Rumble Fish*.

In February 1983, Zoetrope Studios was living on a bank loan, which Coppola was struggling to pay, and the bank was losing patience. Since his personal finances are tied closely to the company, it is not surprising that his home telephone was turned off for a year because he could not pay the bill. Yet Francis Coppola remains undaunted. "You can't be an artist and be safe," he said recently.

Brian De Palma (center) with John Travolta and Nancy Allen on the set of *Blow Out*. PHOTO: United Press International

Brian De Palma

The Wedding Party (1964)
Murder à la Mod (1968)
Greetings (1968)
Hi, Mom! (1970)
Dionysus in '69 (1970)
Get to Know Your Rabbit (1970)
Sisters (1973)

Phantom of the Paradise (1974)
Obsession (1976)
Carrie (1976)
The Fury (1978)
Home Movies (1980)
Dressed to Kill (1980)
Blow Out (1981)

SOME REVIEWERS HAIL Brian De Palma as Master of the Macabre, Prince of Terror, Merchant of Menace, and the Hitchcock of the Seventies. Others call him a cheap imitator and a cold technician who uses blood and violence to manipulate his audiences. De Palma sees himself as a serious filmmaker striving for "the ultimate in filmmaking." He looks at his own films critically again and again, "just to remind myself what was wrong with them. . . . It makes me very aware of what I have to do to grow as a director." And he feels very strongly about his artistic integrity. "I'm devoted to what I'm making," he has said; "what I *am* is up there on the screen."

But Brian De Palma did not always want to direct films. Until he was in college, his "work-oriented, success-oriented" parents were pushing their scientifically inclined son to become a doctor. Meanwhile, his own heart's dream was to go to the moon.

67

De Palma was born on September 11, 1940, in Newark, New Jersey, and grew up in Philadelphia, where his family moved when he was six. He was the youngest of three sons of a politically conservative orthopedic surgeon. De Palma often traces his high tolerance for blood and gore in his films to watching his father in the operating theater as a young boy. He saw him cut open bodies and amputate limbs. When he was seventeen he even did bone transplants himself on animals in his father's lab.

In high school he won second prize at a national science fair and during his senior year designed and built a computer just like the one built by the computer whiz kid in *Dressed to Kill*. He has said, in fact, that "that character in *Dressed to Kill* is me."

De Palma attributes his method of moviemaking—working in a "precise, well-thought-out manner"—in part to his scientific background. He plans his movies shot by shot in advance, including details of camera angle and lighting. "Every shot," he has said, "has a conception behind it." He makes sketches of the scenes and sometimes even takes photographs, then tacks them up around his office. He then moves them around and thinks about them for months, until every scene and every image works in relation to the others. The reason he rejected medicine as a career was that it wasn't "precise enough for me. There seemed to be too much conjecture, too much human error."

At Columbia College, in New York City, he started out majoring in physics (one of his older brothers was a physicist), but he switched to fine arts. He had acted in high school and became involved in college theater as an extracurricular activity. He also became "obsessed" by movies, especially certain movies by Roman Polanski and Alfred Hitchcock. "They seemed terrifying and wonderful to me, and suddenly I knew that I could convey my dreams on the screen. No other art form would do."

He began hanging around the graduate film department and bought himself a secondhand camera. With money from his allowance and from selling everything he owned, including his scientific equipment, he managed to make several short films. The first two of these he describes as "pretentious." But *Wotan's Wake*, a twenty-eight-minute mock horror film he made in his senior year, won every award for a short film that year.

With this recognition, De Palma won a graduate writing fellowship to Sarah Lawrence College. While he was there working on his master's degree and taking a film production course at New York University, he produced, wrote, directed, and edited his first feature, *The Wedding Party*. This satirical film, based on his best friend's wedding, is about the prospective bridegroom's stay at his fiancée's family mansion just before the wedding, and his attempt to escape. It is notable for two things: it is filled with experimental camera and editing techniques that De Palma continues to use—jump cuts, improvised scenes, fast forward, and slow motion; and it starred two new actors—Robert De Niro and Jill Clayburgh.

But it did not bring him even near commercial success. That would take eight more feature films and more than ten years. His first five films were made in New York independently and inexpensively (for $100,000 or less).

When he left Sarah Lawrence, De Palma supported himself by making documentaries for clients including the Museum of Modern Art, the NAACP, and the Treasury Department (*Show Me a Strong Town and I'll Show You a Strong Bank*). He earned enough money to finance *Murder à la Mod*, which he directed, wrote, and edited himself. This is a murder story told from the points of view of three characters, reflected by three different film styles. Seen through the eyes of a deaf-mute character, for instance, the story is a silent comedy. In typical self-criticism, De Palma said several years later, "It didn't work because nobody cared about the characters, and the story was so complicated."

His next two films, *Greetings* and *Hi, Mom!*, were "youth

films," attacking establishment targets. De Palma describes them as statements "of what was going on in my life and the lives around me at that period." He made *Greetings* while he was in a "new talent" program run by Universal Studios. He was hired to write, he said, but nobody read the scripts he sent in. The administrator of the program, who was equally frustrated, wrote the script for *Greetings* with him and raised the money to produce it. They shot it in two weeks with a crew of eight friends, relatives, and film students. The film, which takes its title from the salutation on draft notices, follows three boys around the country—a draft dodger, a Kennedy assassination buff, and a porno artist/filmmaker (Robert De Niro).

Although many critics found the satire "unfunny," it won De Palma a Silver Bear Award in Berlin and made more than $1 million. It also was his first film to be distributed nationally, and De Palma was taken up by the media for a while. But he soon began to feel that he was being used. "I found myself a guest on the 'Joe Franklin Show,' talking about revolution and nudity, and nobody cared about what I said. I was filling up space to sell headache pills."

Hi, Mom! was a kind of sequel, with Robert De Niro returning from the Vietnam War. It made fun of white liberals, black militants, and voyeuristic moviemakers. Critics generally found it sharper and funnier than *Greetings*, but the film didn't do well at the box office. De Palma criticizes it for being "too unintegrated . . . so loose that we had to find a shape for it in the editing room."

While he was finishing *Hi, Mom!*, De Palma filmed an environmental theater production called *Dionysus in '69*, which was based on Euripides' *The Bacchae*. He financed it himself because he was "floored by the emotional power of it" and thought it should be preserved. To do that, he conceived and edited it entirely as a split screen, a technique he has made his own. One side showed the play, the other the reaction and involvement of the audience. The film was praised but made no money.

Editing that split screen took De Palma about a year, and *Dionysus in '69* was the last film he edited alone. He likes to have an editor put together the film as it is being shot so that he can add any missing pieces. He also likes to get another person's responses. Since De Palma's films are so thoroughly planned, he is losing very little personal control. He usually works with the same editor, Paul Hirsch. "As we progress from picture to picture, he almost knows exactly what I have in mind," De Palma has said. "When he gets the footage back, he knows my storyboards and lays it out just like that."

In spite of his feelings about the establishment and his experience with the media, De Palma said after *Hi, Mom!*, "I don't want to make $100,000 movies in back rooms all my life. I'm interested in making my work as good as possible, and if I can put myself into a really heavyweight situation, I'm going to do it."

His reputation as a director with a savage sense of humor finally got him his first shot at Hollywood—one that set him back six years and created permanent feelings of bitterness and suspicion. Warner Brothers hired De Palma to direct *Get to Know Your Rabbit*, the film debut of the comedian Tom Smothers. The film is about a computer executive who drops out to become a tap-dancing magician. De Palma began to have trouble with his star because Smothers didn't like the character he played. Smothers wanted him to be more aggressive, and he was the one who had the influence with the studio. De Palma finally walked away from the picture when Smothers refused to reshoot some scenes. The film was delayed for two years while a Warners executive edited it, and then it flopped.

"I learned from my *Rabbit* experience that you have to be in complete control of a situation," De Palma has said. Meanwhile,

Hollywood had learned that he was a "difficult" director, and he was out of work for a year, until he got independent financing for *Sisters*.

De Palma's next three films—*Sisters*, *Phantom of the Paradise*, and *Obsession*—were all low-budget (about $1.5 million) independent productions, and none of them received very good reviews. But they moved him into the horror/suspense genre where he was ultimately to be most successful. "The reason I like the genre," he has said, "is because you can work in a sort of pure cinematic form. That is why Hitchcock likes it, too. It's all images, and your storytelling is entirely through images and not people talking to each other." He has described his craft as "scaring people with films that are both amusing and more and more visual."

Sisters is the story of Siamese twins, a murder, and a girl reporter who becomes involved. Almost eight years earlier De Palma had seen a photograph in *Life* magazine of a pair of Russian Siamese twins, one smiling, one scowling. "This strong visual image started the whole idea in my mind." His twist is that the sweet sister and the vicious sister turn out to be the same person. When they are separated, one twin dies and the other incorporates her personality.

Although *Sisters* grossed more than $4 million, De Palma had really made it for himself, in order to "develop as a director." "Most of my movies before were sort of cold, intellectual, and satiric," he has said, "and certain parts were good, but there was no structure. . . . This movie was a conscious attempt to tell a story, to involve the audience with the characters, to work in a very cinematic style."

Sisters was the first film for which De Palma was accused of borrowing from Alfred Hitchcock, especially from *Rear Window*. In both films, a reporter witnesses a murder and is unable to persuade anyone to believe the story. Critics also pointed to similar themes—voyeurism, sexual guilt, violence with Freudian overtones—and similar techniques such as involving the audience with a character and then killing him off, using humor to release tension, and a flashy camera style. De Palma even enticed Hitchcock's longtime composer Bernard Herrmann out of retirement to write the score for this film.

He admits that *Sisters* was "obviously influenced by Hitchcock," but insists that "it had a life of its own." Hitchcock, he has said, "is a textbook of film grammar and counterpoint. He's used every kind of visual connection in cinema, yet he's impossible to imitate." De Palma sees his own films as "much more romantic" than Hitchcock's. "I kind of temper my imagery with romantic music, emotionality, and slow motion."

With his next film, *Phantom of the Paradise*, De Palma moved deeper into his chosen genre. The Paradise is a rock palace. It is haunted by a composer whose music was stolen by an evil entrepreneur who has made a pact with the devil. De Palma chose this setting because "the rock world is so stylized and expressionistic to begin with, that it would be a perfect environment in which to tell old horror tales." He had observed the increasing use of horror and violence in acts like the Rolling Stones and Alice Cooper, and wanted to show what that said about contemporary culture.

The violence in this film—when, for instance, the composer's face is crushed in a record presser—drew criticism, as did the bloody murder in *Sisters* and scenes in all his later films. De Palma has answered that "because of my very sort of formalistic training, I sometimes go for what is the strongest, most vivid color on the palette, which in the case of movies is violence."

For *Obsession*, De Palma again used Bernard Herrmann's music. And the story is very close to that of Hitchcock's film *Vertigo*. A man (Cliff Robertson) obsessed with his wife (Genevieve Bujold), who was kidnapped and killed, believes he finds her again in another woman, who turns out to be his daughter. The complex plot is a plan by the man's evil business partner to take over both shares of their real-estate company. Some critics saw the film as a poor copy, but De Palma said that it was another filmmaking assignment he had given himself; he wanted to try to create an intense romantic relationship between two characters.

His next film was a professional turning point for De Palma. Though *Carrie*'s budget was still small (less than $2 million), it was the first film since *Rabbit* that he'd made for a major studio (United Artists); it received good reviews from respectable critics; and two of the actors—Sissy Spacek (Carrie) and Piper Laurie (her mother in the film) were nominated for Academy Awards.

The script was adapted from a novel about a young girl who has telekinetic power—the ability to move objects with her mind. Carrie is being raised by her puritanical, religiously fanatic mother and is an outcast in her high school.

A sympathetic classmate, Sue Snell (Amy Irving), arranges a date for Carrie for the senior prom with handsome, blond Tommy Ross, her own boyfriend. Unknown to her, Chris (Nancy Allen), another classmate, plans a nasty trick to ruin this dream for Carrie. She and her boyfriend (John Travolta) rig the election so that Carrie is voted queen of the prom. Then, when she is standing on the stage wearing her crown, they release a bucket of pig's blood on her from above.

In her fury, Carrie uses her telekinetic power to wreak vengeful destruction all around her—tables overturn, hoses unfurl and blast streams of water, bodies fly. Finally, as she walks out, the room is consumed by fire.

Carrie returns to a house lit by hundreds of candles. Her mothers stands ready with a knife to kill her witch daughter. Instead, Carrie galvanizes all the blades in the house to crucify her mother against a wall and then shuts herself in a closet as the house goes up in flames.

The religious imagery in the film came easily to De Palma. Although he and his brothers were raised as Protestants and went to Quaker schools, the Catholic atmosphere of his father's

Italian-American family "made an indelible impression." Memories from family weddings and funerals—"all those grandparents hovering about and all those candles!"—provided him with "mysterious or terrifying images."

De Palma saw *Carrie* as a culmination of his development so far: "I sort of put everything in *Carrie*," he has said. "I had the romantic story between Tommy Ross and Carrie White; I had all the visual suspense elements; and I was using everything I knew, including comedy and improvisation, from all the other pictures I had made." He also used difficult camera and editing techniques. It took him weeks and weeks to cut the prom scene because he had extended the suspense with slow motion. He spent more weeks cutting the destruction scene into split screen, with Carrie on one side and the flying objects on the other. Otherwise he would have had to cut back and forth between the two again and again. (In reviewing the film for himself later, he was dissatisfied with the effect and concluded that the split screen was a distraction here.)

He was satisfied, however, with the audience's response to the surprise ending. In a dream, Sue goes to the spot where Carrie is buried. As she lays down her flowers, a bloody hand suddenly springs from the earth to grab her. "Never have I seen an audience so universally affected. . . . It gives you real sense of satisfaction when you've emotionally caught up your audience. It's something I've never quite been able to do before."

Carrie was also a major turning point, personally, for the shy, introverted boy who had grown up to be called "the coldest hot director in town." He had told an interviewer in 1973, "I'm almost completely oblivious to my surroundings. I have no desire to own anything. I've never married and don't want to marry. The outside world means little or nothing to me. I'm completely obsessed with film. Everything meaningful is right here in my head, behind my eyes."

There was, in fact, no one woman in his life. He had dated

Margot Kidder when she was starring in *Sisters* and was reported to have had an "intense" relationship with Genevieve Bujold (*Obsession*). But it was a young actress who failed to get the part of Carrie who changed his mind.

De Palma cast Nancy Allen as Chris, Carrie's chief tormentor, because he likes to cast against type, and the contrast between the character's mean nature and Allen's sweet appearance appealed to him. During the filming she thought he didn't like her because he was never particularly friendly. But that is just his style, which he describes as being "very professional." He explained: "I come to the set and am very detached. I'm very much involved in making sure the cinematic design is correct, and I'm trying to think of new ideas. I don't sit there and chat it up with everybody, or pat people on the back."

Nevertheless, she took him up three months later on an open invitation to the cast to visit the studio and watch one of their scenes being edited. That visit turned into a three-year long-distance romance (he was in New York; she was in Los Angeles). Then, on January 12, 1979, they invited fifteen friends over for a party. De Palma assigned a student to film the guests' reactions as they learned that it was a surprise wedding reception.

Allen describes her husband as "very loving and warm" and "*not* a very weird person." They live a quiet life (which they have said will someday include children) in a brownstone in Greenwich Village. Since their marriage, Allen has appeared in all of De Palma's films. In 1980, after *Home Movies*, they separated for a while. "It was just too much togetherness," she said. But after three months, they were back together again, personally and professionally.

After *Carrie*, De Palma was naturally sent piles of similar scripts. He chose to make *The Fury*, which is about two telekinetic teenagers kidnapped by mysterious scientists for use as secret weapons. The story is based on the search of the father of one of them (played by Kirk Douglas) for his son. The film begins and ends with killings.

De Palma thought at the time that he was doing the film for sound reasons. The script had the potential of being visually interesting. "When you're dealing with the interior of someone's mind," he has said, "you can do all sorts of stylized things." And he was given enough time and money ($6.5 million, his biggest budget) to come up with "elaborate cinematic ideas." He was also still teaching himself the art of filmmaking, and he wanted the challenge of making an action picture.

Now he sees *The Fury* as a mistake, and in part he blames his old enemy, Hollywood: "In this business success can be even more destructive than failure, because it can isolate you and leave you surrounded by film people talking about deals and budgets and percentage points, and so you yourself begin to forget what you want to do. Because you have some big star and a terrific deal, you forget to worry about whether this is a movie you should really make."

Although the film was popular at the box office, many reviewers found the story silly and confused and felt that De Palma had used camera tricks for their own sake. He denied that charge and explained, as an example, why he used slow motion for the killing of Hester, a sympathetic character. He wanted to increase the drama and also to convey her point of view: "She's happy and exhilarated and then *pow!* the car hits her." His own evaluation was: "The story and script were way too complicated, and a complicated style such as mine on top of that made it impossible to follow."

In 1978, just as De Palma was getting a firm foothold in Hollywood, he decided to leave commercial filmmaking to teach a course in feature production to fifteen students at Sarah Lawrence College. He taught them how to make a low-budget movie from start to finish: "I wanted to prove that it still can be done." He said that he was considered an aberration in the business, because "a hot director simply doesn't take off two years to do such a thing." But for him it was a relief. He has said, "I was, in a way, going back to my roots, working the way I used to work when I was their age—and at the same time escaping from all those industry types who can turn you inside out."

The film he made with his students is called *Home Movies*. It is a farce about a serious teenage boy who takes home movies of his family. De Palma has described it as "the mad story of a lunatic family" and has also claimed that it is about his own family. It took twice as long to make as a normal feature would have because De Palma had to explain how to do everything—from writing the script to getting financing ($350,000).

Although the list of investors besides De Palma included Steven Spielberg, George Lucas, and Kirk Douglas (who played a role in *Home Movies*), the filmmakers were unable to get a major distributor. Instead, UA Classics, a division of United Artists for films with specialized appeal, distributed it. De Palma complained that the reason the film did poorly was that UA did not spend enough money on promotion, and he even put up some of his own.

De Palma's next two films were commercial movies with large budgets: *Dressed to Kill* cost $7.5 million and *Blow Out* cost $18 million. He wrote both scripts himself, and Nancy Allen played leading roles. She was a high-class call girl in the first film and a small-time prostitute in the second.

Dressed to Kill is about the murder of a middle-aged woman (played by Angie Dickinson), after she is picked up by a man in a museum, and the tracking down of the murderer by her teenage son—an electronics whiz—and a call girl who found the body. De Palma has said of it, "I let my subconscious fears swim to the surface"—fears of what can happen besides sex when you get picked up; of being alone on a subway platform, in an elevator, in your own bathroom.

He has also said, "To me, *Dressed to Kill* is a distillation of all the suspense forms. . . . This story is the most structured of all those I've done. . . . It's a pure study in style—nothing but style. There's almost no dialogue. It's not so much a departure as an evolving of my form and style. The form is the content." The only sound in the long museum pickup scene, for instance, is that of footfalls on the hard floor.

The film got ecstatic reviews from many major critics, although it also elicited criticisms familiar by now to De Palma. Andrew Sarris in the *Village Voice* called it a "shamefully straight steal from *Psycho*, among other things." De Palma uses the famous shower scene and also the psychiatrist explaining the killer's psychosis—in this case, a moralistic transvestite (Michael Caine) punishing promiscuous women.

Some critics objected to the violence in the film. Blood pours through shower curtains and an elevator, and, in fact, De Palma had to re-edit and cut in order to get an R rating rather than an X. Others saw such devices as the split screens, super slow motion, jump cuts, overhead crane shots, and a screen within the screen as style for its own sake.

For his next film, De Palma chose to do a character study. Looking for a new challenge, he decided to try to correct what he saw as his weakness as a director. "I'm usually so involved in the visual storytelling," he has said, "that the slow rising and falling of the character's relationships just don't interest me." This is evident in the fact that his rough cuts, unlike those of most directors, are usually shorter than the final version. "I throw all the character scenes out," he once said. "The film runs like a crazy windup toy. Then I start building them back in again."

He got the idea for *Blow Out* after he did *Carrie*. His sound-effects man on that film went on vacation, and De Palma noticed that he took his tape recorder along. "I began to wonder what sort of man chooses that profession," he said. In *Blow Out*, Jack (John Travolta), the sound-effects man for a film company that makes sexy thrillers, is innocently collecting sounds (an owl, the wind) one night when he hears a tire blow out and sees a car crash into the water. He rescues a young woman from the car, but the man with her (a candidate for President) is dead. Listening to his tape later, he realizes that the blowout was actually a gunshot, and he determines to solve the dangerous mystery.

The film was criticized for putting too much emphasis on style and not enough on logic. But in the *New Yorker*, Pauline Kael, a devout De Palma fan, called it "a great movie." In her review, she wrote, "For the first time, De Palma goes inside his central character . . . and stays inside . . . *Blow Out* is the first movie in which De Palma has stripped away the cackle and the glee. . . . He's playing it straight, and asking you—trusting you—to respond." She also wrote, "This is the first film he has made about the things that really matter to him."

One of these things is his pessimistic political vision. "I have this real sense of the effects of the capitalistic society in which everything is done for the sake of profit," he said recently. "It's totally attacked the moral fiber, and I'm very interested in how it affects the lives of people who go up against it—*Blow Out* is very much about that. I don't think the system can be changed. It's too strong and powerful—it just engulfs you."

George Lucas on location with *Raiders of the Lost Ark*. PHOTO: Courtesy of Lucasfilm, Ltd.

George Lucas

THX–1138 (1971)
American Graffiti (1973)
Star Wars (1977)
The Empire Strikes Back (1980, executive producer)
Raiders of the Lost Ark (1981, executive producer)
Return of the Jedi (1983, executive producer)

GEORGE LUCAS doesn't look like a prodigy. He is a short, almost painfully shy young man, who usually dresses in jeans and sneakers and hides behind glasses and a bushy black beard. Yet the film critic Stephen Farber wrote that "at twenty-eight" Lucas was "already one of the world's master directors." At thirty-six, according to *Fortune* magazine, he was "the most successful executive in the beleaguered motion-picture business." What is prodigious about George Lucas is his ability to change the ordinary stuff of his own childhood into movies that capture the imagination of millions of children and adults.

What was the stuff of that childhood? George Lucas was born in the rural town of Modesto, California, on May 14, 1944. He has described his family as "middle middle class." His father owned a stationery and office supply store and farmed in his spare time. George and his three sisters were raised on a walnut ranch just outside town.

Lucas didn't grow up as a movie fan. There were few theaters in Modesto and when he went to the movies, he has said, "I really didn't pay much attention. I was usually going to look for girls and goof off." Instead he listened to rock 'n' roll, watched Flash Gordon and the Republic adventure serials on television, and hung around his father's store reading the comic books on the racks. He still listens to rock 'n' roll and has a giant collection of 78 rpms from the fifties and sixties. He also continues to read science fiction and now collects both books and art works in that area.

As a teenager, Lucas has said, "I was a hell-raiser." He "lived, ate, breathed cars! That was everything for me." With his small, souped-up Fiat, he drove around Modesto like the teenagers in *American Graffiti*. He got a job rebuilding cars at a foreign-car garage and worked on pit crews at races around the country. He even won some trophies and dreamed of being a racing car driver.

Then two days before he was to graduate from high school (with a "D-plus, plus average"), Lucas's car was hit by a driver going ninety miles an hour. He was thrown clear and broke only two bones, but his lungs were crushed, and he spent three months in the hospital. "Before the accident," he has said, "I never used to think. Afterward, I realized I had to plan if I was ever to be happy."

His first decision was to become a serious student. He enrolled as a social science major at Modesto Junior College, and he began to paint. When he graduated, he wanted to go to art school, but his father was afraid he would become a beatnik and refused to pay his tuition. Lucas was working at the time as a mechanic on a racing car for Haskell Wexler, the famous cinematographer. Lucas had taken still pictures for car racers and played around with a friend's 8-millimeter camera, but he "didn't really know what films were all about." Nevertheless, Wexler whetted his interest and helped him get into the University of

Southern California film school, which his father considered respectable.

He planned to study still photography and animation. Instead, he discovered Fellini, Truffaut, Godard, and the underground filmmakers of San Francisco. "Movies replaced my love for cars. . . . When I finally discovered film, I really fell madly in love with it, ate it and slept it twenty-four hours a day."

Lucas was a star student at USC, sweeping the awards at film festivals. He made eight movies while he was in school because he was willing to break rules, like buying extra footage for what were supposed to be class projects. He believes that "nobody's *ever* going to let anybody make a movie. You have to go out and do it!"

This, he has said, is his philosophy of life and "one of the main thrusts in all the films . . . the fact that if you apply yourself and work real hard, you can get what you want accomplished. Your only limitations are your own willingness to do whatever you want to do. In *THX* . . . the whole film, really, is the analogy that we're in cages and the doors are open. We just don't want to leave . . . . *American Graffiti*'s saying the same thing . . . that you have to go out into the world and make something of yourself—no matter how frightening that is. And it recurs in *Star Wars* with Luke wanting something, but not wanting it enough to break the rules and say, 'Okay, I'm going to do it.'" In *The Empire Strikes Back* and *Return of the Jedi* (the third movie in the series), "It's the same thing but more inward than outward. More personal."

Lucas's first films were "very abstract—tone poems, visual. . . . I didn't want to know about stories and plot and characters." One, *The Emperor*, is a documentary about a disc jockey, a subject he returned to in *American Graffiti*. *THX–1138*, an award-winning exercise in lighting, was the basis of his first feature.

In film school, editing had been Lucas's first love, and he still says it's "what I can really sit and do and lose track of time and enjoy myself." (His former wife Marcia is a well-respected film editor, who has worked on his films as well as those of Scorsese and others.) But the jobs he got after graduation as a grip, cameraman, assistant editor, and editor convinced him that he wanted to direct. "I really didn't like people telling me how to do this and how to do that . . . carrying out someone else's ideas that I really didn't think were so great."

Lucas won a scholarship from Warner Brothers to watch the shooting of *Finian's Rainbow*. On a similar scholarship, he had watched Carl Foreman direct *McKenna's Gold*, a conventional Hollywood film. Lucas made an award-winning behind-the-scenes film, supposedly about that experience, but really more about the desert where the film took place than about the film itself. He had been bored watching Foreman and wasn't eager to do something like that again. But this time it would be different. The director of *Finian's Rainbow* was Francis Coppola, who would become for Lucas both friend and mentor.

Lucas ended up staying with Coppola as a "general do-everything" for his next film, *The Rain People*. The forty-minute documentary he made about it, called *Filmmaker*, is considered one of the best films on filmmaking. He then became a vice-president of Coppola's production company, Zoetrope, and in his own words was Coppola's "right hand for ten years." Yet, according to Lucas, no two people could be more different. "Francis spends every day jumping off a cliff and hoping he's going to land okay. My main interest is security. . . . But the goals we have in mind are the same. We want to make movies and be free from the yoke of the studios."

Lucas has said that he learned "the way I make movies" from Coppola. It was Coppola who forced him to become a writer, though he was never good in English in school and had done terribly in scriptwriting classes. Even now, he finds writing an "agonizing" experience.

But Coppola insisted that he add a plot to *THX* so that American Zoetrope could produce it as a feature. It took four drafts and several collaborations to create the story of a man in a dehumanized, drug-oriented, future world, who tries to escape. Robert Duvall, his head shaved, played the lead.

Coppola produced *THX* for Warner Brothers on a tiny budget, which allowed the director only $15,000. The slick-looking film was shot entirely on location. The crew and all the equipment traveled in a van to the twenty-two unlikely filming sites—the unfinished tunnels of the San Francisco subway system, for instance, where a jet car and jet motorcycle chase took place.

The Warners executives who saw the rough cut hated it, and Lucas blames them for the lack of publicity the film got. But he was angrier still that they cut a few minutes without his approval.

THX got mixed reviews but brought George Lucas a cult following. It was chosen for an award by a radical directors' group at the Cannes Film Festival. When Warners refused to pay their fare, Lucas and his wife packed their backpacks and spent their last $2,000 to get there.

George Lucas's second film, *American Graffiti*, seems completely different from his first. "*THX* is very much the way that I am as a filmmaker," he has said. "*American Graffiti* is very much the way I am as a person." *THX* earned Lucas a reputation as a very cold science fiction director, and he wasn't being offered any scripts. Coppola told him he had to prove that he could write something warm and human. What he came up with was a script for a "rock 'n' roll cruising movie." He wrote it himself ("kicking and screaming"), but he asked two friends from film school to rewrite it. "The scenes are mine," he has said. "The dialogue is theirs."

Lucas spent a year and a half trying to sell *American Graffiti* to a studio. Universal Studios finally took it on the condition that Coppola agree to be the coproducer. Lucas was given a budget of about $700,000. Of that, his fee was $20,000 and he spent $80,000 on forty-two rock songs that made up the sound track. The opening shot is a closeup of the markings on a radio dial and the background is a steady stream of fifties radio music with fragments from a disc jockey's (Wolfman Jack's) monologue.

The film interweaves the stories of four young men on the eve of their graduation from a small-town high school in Northern California in 1962 (the same year Lucas graduated). They are all at turning points, which are played out during the twelve hours between dusk and daylight, mainly in their ever-cruising cars and at Mel's Burger City Drive-In.

Two of them—Steve and Curt—are supposed to leave the next morning for college in the East. Steve is class president, freckle-faced and all-American. His cheerleader girl friend doesn't want him to go. Curt, the class intellectual, is picked up by a gang of hoods and forced to carry out their demands. Once he has proved himself, he decides to search out the real Wolfman Jack. Terry, with his buckteeth and freckles, is an outsider, who never can quite keep up with the others because he doesn't have a car. Tonight he borrows one and gets a girl. Finally, John Milner is the future. Five years older than the others, he is still cruising in his "piss-yellow deuce coupe." He wins the climactic drag race but realizes that he is over the hill.

Having learned from Coppola the importance of actors, Lucas spent four months casting *American Graffiti*. For twelve to four-teen hours a day, six days a week, he interviewed everyone, giving them five or ten minutes apiece. "I like to get someone who I feel more or less *is* the character," he has said, "and then utilize his own personal capacity and personality traits." He worked the same way on *Star Wars*, a film that took three months to cast.

Yet, the actual directing of actors seems to make him slightly uncomfortable. Richard Dreyfuss, who played Curt, joked that it was three weeks before he knew that his director spoke English. According to Coppola, Lucas leads his actors indirectly: "He constructs his scenes so specifically, or narrowly . . . that everything comes out more or less the way he sees it." Lucas himself believes that he has an advantage as a director because "I know exactly what I want. . . . Life becomes for me whatever it is that I'm making a movie about for the year or two that I'm making it. So, when the time comes for me to tell an actor to do this or that, there is no question in my mind what he should do."

Lucas found directing *American Graffiti* a "rather horrendous experience." Since the film takes place at night, it had to be shot at night—twenty-eight nights, shooting from 9:00 P.M. to 5:00 A.M. At first Lucas tried to be both director and cinematographer, as he had been on *THX*, but he couldn't do it. He hired two cameramen and then called in his old friend Haskell Wexler to help him get the look he wanted—"all yellow and red and orange . . . very much like a carnival."

The studio executives again hated his film. They wanted to sell it as a TV movie; they wanted to change the title to *Another Slow Night in Modesto*. According to Lucas, half of them didn't know what *American Graffiti* meant; they thought it sounded like an Italian movie or a movie about feet. They did release it finally, but in a form that violated Lucas's vision: they cut about five minutes and did not use the stereophonic sound that was designed for it. (When Lucas re-released the film in 1978, he corrected both of these defects.)

To Universal's surprise, the film became the studio's biggest hit of all time and one of the most popular films of the 1970s. It was nominated for five Academy Awards, and the screenplay won awards from the New York Film Critics Circle and the National Society of Film Critics.

Almost all reviewers praised the technical achievements of *American Graffiti*—the cinematography, editing, and acting. But they divided over whether it is a serious film or just superficial nostalgia. Lucas has said that it is not about the sixties, but about change, "about teenagers accepting the fact that they have to leave home. It's about the end of an era, how things can't stay the same." As one boy in the film says to another, "You can't stay seventeen forever."

Lucas does acknowledge the film's autobiographical roots. "It all happened to me, but I sort of glamorized it. I spent four years of my life cruising the main street of my home town. . . . I started as Terry the toad, but then I went on to be John Milner, the local drag race champion, and then I became Curt Henderson, the intellectual who goes off to college. They were all composite characters, based on my life, and on the lives of friends of mine."

Success didn't change George Lucas's life. With typical generosity, he gave part of the profits from the film to the main actors and continued to live frugally on his wife's salary as an editor. He invested most of the money he got in his next project, a "space fantasy" for children called *Star Wars*. He had had the idea in mind before he started shooting *American Graffiti*, and he began researching and writing it as soon as the film was done.

Lucas had two reasons for wanting to make this film. As a director, he wanted the challenge of making a real movie, one with plot and characters that would require the use of sound stages with sets, "the way they used to make movies." As a filmmaker, he wanted to create a modern fairy tale. "As a student of anthropology," he has said, "I feel strongly about the role myths and fairy tales play in setting up young people for the way they're supposed to handle themselves in society." He thinks that "young people don't have a fantasy life anymore, not the way *we* did. All they've got is Kojak and Dirty Harry. There're all these kids running around, wanting to be killer cops."

While he was writing, Lucas read books on mythology, fantasy, and anthropology. This he combined with the "flotsam and jetsam from the period when I was twelve years old. All the books and films and comics that I liked when I was a child."

After two and a half years of full-time work, he had written four different versions of the script. The first version, which he rejected, centered completely on the robots. The final version consisted of six films in two trilogies. (He added a third after the success of *Star Wars* and has said that the full cycle should take about twenty years to film.) Although humans now have the central roles, only the robots R2-D2 and C-3PO appear in all the episodes. "In effect, the story will be told through their eyes," Lucas has said.

He chose to begin with episode four of *Star Wars*, *The New Hope*, because it has the most action. There are lightsaber fights between Luke Skywalker and Darth Vader and spaceship chases and battles, all set against a war between the Imperial and Rebel forces "in a galaxy far away."

Lucas showed his script to almost every major studio before 20th Century-Fox was willing to take a chance on it and agree to his demand for control over final cut, merchandising, and publicity. He was given a budget of $8.5 million (he eventually spent $9.5 million) and a cast and crew of 950, compared with the forty he had had before. Yet he considers *Star Wars* a "real low-budget movie."

He had had to pare down his original budget estimate of $18 million, and, as a result, the film is full of compromises. He cut out over a hundred special-effects shots. New sets were made from old sets. Space weapons were made out of cut-down machine guns. The robots didn't work right at first. The original R2-D2 couldn't go more than three feet without running into something. (Extra footage was shot later with a rebuilt robot for some movie shots to be used at the beginning.) Even the cantina scene, in which Luke (Mark Hamill) and Ben Kenobi (Alec Guinness) hire Han Solo (Harrison Ford) and Chewbacca from among a roomful of bizarre, otherworldly creatures, is only a shadow of what was in Lucas's imagination. The designer fell sick, and the studio wouldn't give Lucas enough money to have someone fully complete it. "The film is about 25 percent of what I wanted it to be," he has said.

Lucas formed his own company, Industrial Light and Magic, to supply *Star Wars* with its 365 special-effects shots. These shots, some of which combined from five to thirty elements, required models, computers, special cameras, mattes, and blue screens. They took up almost half the budget and were visible for half the running time of the film. ILM also created every sound in *Star Wars*, since a door slamming or a foot falling on the planet Tatooine couldn't be the same as that sound on earth. An ordinary film has two hundred sound units; *Star Wars* has two thousand.

The special-effects company would be used for Lucas's future films. One-fifth of *The Empire Strikes Back* was shot by ILM without actors, as were some of the escapes and supernatural aspects of *Raiders of the Lost Ark*, and most of the 942 special effects in *Return of the Jedi*. ILM is now a big, expensively equipped company that does work for other filmmakers as well and is noted for its glossy professionalism.

The team Lucas hired for ILM was relatively young and inexperienced. He knew exactly the effects he wanted for *Star Wars*, and he was looking for people who would produce them without question. Then he worked very closely with them, spending months with the artists who sculpted C-3PO's face and the technicians who developed R2-D2's vocabulary of beeps, whistles, sighs, and eeks. He described C-3PO as "an overly emotional, fussy robot." He didn't want his face to be inhuman; he wanted it to be one people could respond to.

The whole film was meticulously drawn out in advance on storyboards. Lucas also put together World War II and Korean

War movie footage to show how he wanted the air fights between the spaceships to look.

With *Star Wars*, as with his earlier films, Lucas could not delegate responsibility. "If I left anything for a day, it would fall apart, and it's purely because I set it up that way," he has said. By the end of the filming, he was exhausted and depressed. He was also permanently soured on directing. "I spent all my time yelling and screaming at people, and I have never had to do that before." He has also said, "I've discovered what I knew all along: I am not a film director. I'm a filmmaker. A film director is somebody who directs people—large operations. I like to sit down behind a camera and shoot pretty pictures and then cut them together and watch the magic come as I combine images and tell stories."

Lucas expected the movie to be "moderately successful," and he flew off to Hawaii with his wife for a vacation before he could find out whether or not it was doing well. In fact, *Star Wars* was the most lucrative movie up to that time, grossing about $500 million. Lucas got between $22 and $26 million for himself ($12 million after taxes). It could have been more, but he gave away one-quarter of his profits to the actors, people on the set, and his office employees. As for himself and his wife (the couple Francis Coppola once called "country mice"), he has said, "On a personal level it doesn't mean much of a change. . . . Once you have a car and a house there's not much more you can do except eat out more."

Star Wars opened to almost unanimous praise from reviewers of widely different tastes and ages and won seven Academy Awards. Reviewers called it "magnificent," "grand," "glorious," and "exhilarating," even while admitting that it was pure escapism.

After *Star Wars*, George Lucas stated his intent never to direct again. "Now I can go back to what I want to do," he has said, "experimental, abstract kinds of things, working with pure form."

His plan was to support this by supervising sequels to *American Graffiti* and *Star Wars*.

True to his word, in part at least, he became a producer and chairman of the board of Lucasfilm Limited. In 1981, he closed the doors on directing and resigned from the Directors Guild of America, the Writers Guild of America, and the Academy of Motion Picture Arts and Sciences. These resignations came in the wake of a $250,000 fine for putting Irvin Kershner's credit at the end rather than the beginning of *The Empire Strikes Back*, even though the director had consented to the end credit.

As a producer, Lucas has said, "I might have more decisions to make, but the pressures seem less enormous." His first production was *More American Graffiti*. He developed the story but was not directly involved in the production, and it was a critical and box office failure, Lucas's only one. Then Lucas used almost all of his earnings from *Star Wars* as collateral to borrow the $22 million he needed to produce episode five of *Star Wars*, *The Empire Strikes Back* (the film ended up costing $30 million). Since he was financing it, he could keep all the profits after the costs of distribution.

The Empire Strikes Back grossed about $350 million, but the critical consensus was that it is not as much fun as the original *Star Wars*. It is difficult to separate Lucas's contributions to the film from those of the director, Irvin Kershner. At one time Lucas said, "It's truly Kershner's movie." At another, he said, "I'm the boss." In fact, Lucas wrote the story (though not the script), created the storyboards, was sent black-and-white videotapes daily, gave technical advice, oversaw the editing and special effects, and spent six weeks polishing the sound and images in a sound-mixing room. Kershner himself admits to working in Lucas's mold: "I was trying to keep the convention that George Lucas set up where you stay with no scene very long. . . and where the editorial rhythm is in a way more important than the camera moves or the actors saying their lines."

Steven Spielberg played a similar role as director of Lucas's next project, *Raiders of the Lost Ark*. "The movie stylistically is very loyal to George's concept and impulse," he said. "It's as if I slipped into George's shoes and directed the picture as George might have . . . rather than imposing my style onto the project." He also said he learned creative shortcuts from Lucas—"how to give the audience the eyeful with *illusions* of grandeur." Lucas collaborated on the script for this film, helped with the special effects, did the editing, and at Spielberg's invitation also went on location.

Raiders won praise as escapist entertainment. It is a sophisticated adventure movie about an archaeologist-adventurer named Indiana Jones (Harrison Ford), who is in pursuit of a supernatural treasure, the lost Ark of the Covenant. It is based on a story Lucas wrote ten years earlier, and he has already mapped out story lines for four planned sequels. One of these, *Indiana Jones: The Temple of Doom*, is in production. "What interests me here," Lucas has said, "is this fascinating character. If I could be a dream figure, I'd be Indy. It's not just that I'm interested in archeology or anthropology. . . . It's that Indy can do *anything*. . . . He's this renegade archeologist and adventurer, but he's also a college professor, and he's got his Cary Grant side."

Lucas was again a looming presence on the set of the next *Star Wars* episode, *Return of the Jedi*. Although he chose another director (Richard Marquand), he wrote the first draft of the script and he has said, "I want these three films to have a unity because it's one story. I knew I had to be here to keep the look of it consistent, the art direction consistent, the technology consistent."

But George Lucas is also a businessman and has to spend time making deals as well as films. "Business is a necessary evil for me now," he said in late 1980. "I'm trying to turn the studio system around. The studios use films they don't have the vaguest idea how to make to earn profits for their shareholders. I'm using my profits to make films." Lucasfilm Limited is a multimillion-dollar entertainment company that concentrates on filmmaking and related merchandising activities, such as selling the dolls, games, and T-shirts made by the fifty or sixty licensees of *Star Wars* and *The Empire Strikes Back*, whose gross retail sales so far have been about $1.5 billion. Lucasfilm employs about 350 people, owns Industrial Light and Magic, and has extensive post-production facilities.

Lucas runs the company tightly but definitely in his own style. Many of the top executives are film school graduates or are at least very knowledgeable about film. His employees work hard but are paid well. He refuses to license his films for use on liquor or cigarettes or toys with sharp edges, and because he himself is a diabetic, he asked the licensee for *Star Wars* chewing gum to offer a sugarless variety.

He also has a vision of a community of filmmakers living and working together. This vision should take form by 1984 on what he calls Skywalker Ranch, a 3,000-acre $20 million enclosure in the Marin County Hills, where all of Lucasfilm except ILM will be moved. Lucas himself designed the main building in a Victorian style, like his own home in a San Francisco suburb. "Writers need privacy," he has said, "and Victorian houses are full of cubbyholes." He has described Skywalker Ranch as "a creative retreat where filmmakers can meet, study, collaborate, write, edit, and experiment with new filmmaking ideas."

George Lucas is a controversial figure right now. He keeps talking about the experimental films that he wants to make—as soon as the ranch is ready. "My ambition," he has said, "is to make movies, but all by myself, to shoot them, cut them, make stuff I want to, just for my own exploration, to see if I can combine images in a certain way. My movies will go back to the way my first films were, which dealt a little more realistically with the human condition." But some critics don't believe him. Stuart Byron, in the *Village Voice*, called him "the most reactionary filmmaker in America," and Pauline Kael, in the *New Yorker*, accused him of being in the toy business and wrote that he is "hooked on the crap of his childhood."

When *Jedi* opened in May 1983, Lucas announced that he was taking a two-year sabbatical from Lucasfilm. A month later he announced the break-up of his thirteen-year marriage. During the sabbatical he plans to read and write, and also to spend time with his two-year-old adopted daughter, for whom he will share custody. Maybe at the end of that time, one side of his genius will have prevailed—the filmmaker side or the toymaker side.

Paul Mazursky

Paul Mazursky

Bob and Carol and Ted and Alice (1969)
Alex in Wonderland (1970)
Blume in Love (1973)
Harry and Tonto (1974)
Next Stop, Greenwich Village (1976)
An Unmarried Woman (1978)
Willie and Phil (1980)
Tempest (1982)

"IN MY TIME," Paul Mazursky has recalled, "we all wanted to be in the theater; movies were a kind of sell-out. I never fantasized that I wanted to direct films." What he did fantasize about was a career as an actor—something he hasn't entirely abandoned. Since he began directing, Mazursky has given himself cameo roles in several of his films and has appeared in two films by other directors—*A Star Is Born* and *A Man, a Woman, and a Bank*. And he has always received good notices.

Paul Mazursky was born Irwin Mazursky in Brownsville, a lower-middle-class Jewish section of Brooklyn, on April 25, 1930. During the depression his father worked as a ditch digger. Later he got a job loading trucks. Mazursky has described his mother as a "very powerful woman with tremendous energy that was not used, not plugged in. So it frizzed all over the joint." (Not unlike the mother in *Next Stop, Greenwich Village*.)

99

It was his grandfather, however, his mother's father, who introduced him to literature and culture. A Russian émigré who ran a candy store down the block, he would play the violin for his grandson and talk about the great Russian writers, whom he had reread in English.

Mazursky's dream of being an actor began in childhood. From the age of twelve, he read every play he could find. He had roles in high-school plays and continued acting at Brooklyn College, where he was a speech therapy and English literature major. During his senior year he starred in an Off-Broadway production and changed his name to Paul. ("I hated the name Irwin from the day I way born. To me, a schnook.")

Then he got his big break—a leading role in *Fear and Desire*, a film about a soldier who goes berserk and the first feature made by the now famous director Stanley Kubrick. "I thought it was the big time. I was paid a hundred dollars a week for a month's work and had a free round trip to California. And I had my Academy Award speech all written out, in which I thanked the dean for giving me a leave of absence to do the picture." But *Fear and Desire* was a flop, and reviewers criticized Mazursky for overacting.

Nevertheless, it made his fantasy of being an actor real; he felt like a professional. After graduation, he moved to Greenwich Village, studied acting with Paul Mann and Lee Strasberg, and waited for another break. It came in 1954, when he was cast as a juvenile delinquent in *The Blackboard Jungle*, a big commercial film.

But his acting career never took hold. About the next five years, he has said, "I almost never had an acting job that lasted as much as three weeks." He spent the rest of his time as a bit actor on television, a nightclub comic, an acting teacher, the director of a unsuccessful Off-Broadway revue, an unpublished short story writer, and a sales clerk in a health food store.

In the late 1950s, Larry Tucker, owner of a club in which

Mazursky had performed, asked him to help start an improvisational comic revue in Los Angeles. Since live TV had dried up by this time in New York, Mazursky agreed. He packed up and left, with his wife and one-year-old daughter.

While he was working with Tucker on this and other revues, Mazursky was also acting and writing on his own. He wrote his own nightclub routines and started writing television scripts, though he was unable to sell any of them. He also wrote a twelve-minute film, *Last Year at Malibu*. It was a parody of the arty New Wave directors, and he dubbed the narration in phony French, Swedish, and Japanese.

In 1963 Mazursky and Tucker were both hired as writers for "The Danny Kaye Show" on TV, where they worked for four years. Although he was making $75,000 a year, Mazursky was unhappy. He continued to act occasionally with a repertory company and, always a film buff, took courses in cutting and editing. He has said of that time, "I knew I wasn't going to try to be an actor anymore or make a living as a comedy writer. I was going to direct films or get out of show business."

During the summers he and Tucker worked toward that goal. First they wrote a screenplay titled *H–Bomb Beach Party*. which was sold but never filmed. Then they wrote *I Love You, Alice B. Toklas*, a comic satire about the romance between a lawyer in his forties and a hippie. It was sold and made into a successful film starring Peter Sellers. This gave them the bargaining power they needed when they peddled their next script, *Bob and Carol and Ted and Alice*. Mazursky could demand—and get—the right to direct and the chance to begin his career as a filmmaker.

All of Mazursky's films have a common theme. He calls them "inner journeys" and "painful comedies." They are satires, but they are gentle, because of his attitude toward his characters and toward life. He writes about what he knows—typically the affluent middle-class America of white, liberal professionals—and he feels compassion for his characters—"because I'm one of them," he explained. "I'm always writing about real people in specific situations," he has said. "The humor in my films comes out of those real situations."

Mazursky takes love seriously, he believes in marriage, and he is basically optimistic. All his films end, he has said, "with the feeling of affirmation—or at least the feeling of the *possibility* of affirmation."

He usually keeps the look of his films simple. The most striking visual element is likely to be the expression on an actor's face. "If the audience is aware of the camera's movement," he has said, "it takes away from the story."

Mazursky's films seem improvisational, although they usually stay very close to the script. "Generally I don't like to shoot improvisation," he has said. "Actors can get hooked on a lot of things that seem like fun at the time but have nothing to do with what I wrote. I want to respect myself as a writer." He does, however, occasionally add nonprofessionals to the cast (like the psychiatrists in several of his films) to give a documentary flavor.

The most consistent criticism of Mazursky's movies is the charge of sentimentality. "I've always defended myself," he has said, "by saying my movies aren't sentimental, they just have sentiment. I feel pity for my characters." He acknowledges, however, that the line between the two is a fine one.

Bob and Carol and Ted and Alice was Mazursky's first look at life-styles. It focused on the West Coast because that was where he was living at the time. He has said that the film is "about the sexual revolution and the problems the middle class has in adjusting to a new freedom." It is the story of a filmmaker and his wife, Bob and Carol (Robert Culp and Natalie Wood), who spend a weekend at an encounter group and return home eager to share their new sexual liberation and openness with their uptight friends, Ted and Alice (Elliott Gould and Dyan Cannon).

At first, when the two couples talk at dinner, it's just talk to Ted and Alice. Ted jokingly confesses his deep feeling that Bob should pick up the check. Later, Bob returns from a business trip and confesses to Carol that he has had a casual affair. It takes her a moment to respond as she now thinks she should. Then she says, "Let me hear about it again. I feel closer to you than I ever have in my whole life." She shares this good news with a bewildered Ted and a horrified Alice.

Mazursky and Tucker got the idea for the film from a picture in *Time* magazine of six people sitting together naked in a tub. The photograph carried the caption, "Couples find joy." But the first draft of the script went very slowly until Mazursky and his wife attended an encounter session themselves. He wrote about their experience, "began to fantasize," and finished the script in five days.

Although Mazursky insisted on directing the film himself, he admitted that he had no technical experience. "What I really had," he has said, "was an instinct for staging because I had directed in the theater and been an actor. So I was able to see, for instance, that in a given scene the actors should not sit on the couch for five pages, so maybe here she should get up, go over to the bar and get a drink, and while she's getting the drink we'll put the camera over her shoulder."

He depended on his crew for technical help, but he always chose where to put the camera. For every shot in his films, Mazursky looks through the viewfinder himself. "You have to. . . . If what the camera sees is off, then your whole vision is off. So how can you work on the iceberg of the movie and leave the tip to someone else?"

Because of his experience as an actor and acting teacher, Mazursky is very comfortable working with actors, and they are comfortable with him. He has always been credited with being able to get wonderful, natural performances. He has said, "I learned something from having acted that's pragmatic—not just say it louder or do it softer. First, you must cast the part well, and then you must have a mutual kind of dialogue with the actor, where you're not afraid to admit to each other when you're stuck." During rehearsals he plays records—"anything that helps make the people more free. . . ." His sets are always relaxed, and between takes he talks and jokes.

Mazursky's acting experience also affects the way he rehearses: "Most directors don't understand the deep process of acting, whereas I know how to get actors to a relaxed place—a place where the revelations start to come. Weeks before the camera rolls, I put people together and rehearse in unsual ways." His rehearsals include going over lines and improvising character, reading the script and trying to understand it together, "then throwing the script away and just letting them talk to each other. Letting the actors trust each other enough to be silly."

He also works through surprise: "I never like to tell my actors too much of what's going on. . . . Otherwise you might get a good result, but it won't go as far as it could." At the end of *Bob and Carol*, for instance, the two couples are finally in bed together at a Las Vegas hotel after Ted has delayed in the bathroom as long as he possibly can. The actors kept asking him what they were going to do. "I really wasn't sure," Mazursky says. "But I could see that if I didn't tell them, it would add to their personal kind of dilemma, so I kept saying, 'Oh, it'll be great. It will all work out.' . . . They were all very weird and very giggly and very strange. It was real; it was happening to them." And, needless to say, the planned orgy never got off the ground.

Bob and Carol and Ted and Alice was chosen to open the New York Film Festival, the first time so clearly commercial a film did so, and it created a great controversy. Some critics found it original and funny, while others complained that it was nothing more than a slick TV situation comedy.

Despite the critical controversy, the film grossed more than $20 million and made Paul Mazursky a millionaire in a year and a half. It gave him the freedom to continue doing what he wanted in his own way. As a result, Mazursky has always had total control of his films. Not a single frame has ever been changed by a studio, and he has a voice in marketing decisions as well.

Rather than direct one of the many scripts sent to him after *Bob and Carol*, Mazursky decided to do another film based on his own background—"The people I know. The world I know. The dreams in my head. The fears in my heart." He even used his own house. This film, *Alex in Wonderland*, is about a director (Donald Sutherland) who hits it big and what happens to him in reality and in his fantasies. He doesn't want to do the scripts he is offered—*Don Quixote* as a Western, *Huckleberry Finn* as a musical, a heart transplant film—but he doesn't know what he wants to do. *Alex in Wonderland* was a critical and box office failure and marked the end of Mazursky's collaboration with Tucker.

Stephen Farber, commenting in the *New York Times*, summarized the critics' response by calling the film "an extreme in narcissistic filmmaking" and a "pop 8½." Mazursky admitted that Fellini (the director of 8½, who actually played a small part in *Alex in Wonderland*) influenced him, but claimed that he wasn't pretending to be Fellini; he "just wanted to be that good." He remains fond of *Alex* as "the infant nobody appreciated."

Mazursky was unemployed for the next two years. He had an idea for the story of an old man and a cat and got money for the first draft of a script, which he wrote with an old friend from New York. But he peddled *Harry and Tonto* around the movie studios for six months and got fourteen rejections.

Dejected, Mazursky and his family went to Europe for six months, and he almost accepted a job directing someone else's film. But at the last moment, in a mere six weeks, he wrote *Blume in Love*, which many critics consider his best film. "It was based," he has said, "on real feelings and problems I'd had with my wife in Rome. We were unhappy, we were arguing a lot. I had strange feelings. Nothing in the movie ever took place, but I guess what I wanted to write was 'What if this woman that I love so much said, "Get out!"'"

He told the story of Steven Blume (George Segal) and his wife Nina (Susan Anspach) in flashbacks. She finds him in bed with his secretary and kicks him out. But he is obsessively in love with her and determined to get her back. "She's the only woman I will ever love," Blume says, "ever. I will die if I don't get her back. I don't want to die. Therefore I will have to get her back." In *Blume in Love*, Mazursky has said, "I wanted to deal with the middle class romantically."

Although the acting in the film was praised, some critics questioned the choice of Susan Anspach rather than an extraordinarily beautiful actress like Ali McGraw, whom the studio originally suggested for the part of Nina. "I deliberately wanted to use someone who was attractive, who tried to make her ordinariness extraordinary. The way middle-class people do," Mazursky has said, defending his choice. He also, consciously or unconsciously, chose an actress who looks strikingly like his wife.

Strangely, for a director who usually treads the same territory, Mazursky rarely uses any of the same cast. "Every part is different," he has said, "and I'm looking for the persona of that character, not just going for talent." Mazursky usually prefers to cast to type, judging less by how actors read for the part than by what he thinks they are like as people. He also has great reservations about using very famous movie stars. "Generally speaking, if you've got a big movie star in the part, the charisma of the movie star becomes greater than the reality of the role."

After the modest success of *Blume in Love*, Mazursky was able to sell *Harry and Tonto*, although the budget was pared down to the bone and he got the lowest possible fee. Yet, in spite of all the studio's hesitation, the film was praised by the critics and made $5 million.

Art Carney also won an Oscar for playing the part of Harry. Mazursky wasn't surprised. "I could tell from sitting and talking with him that he was Harry."

Harry and Tonto is the only Mazursky film critics rarely compare to his life. It is about an old man who is evicted from his New York apartment. He travels across America with his cat, meeting various characters and making disappointing stops at the homes of his three children. Mazursky has said that it is just as personal as his other films. "I got the idea for *Harry and Tonto* when I was forty. When I became forty, I began seriously to think about the fact that I would one day be seventy. When you're twenty, you'll never be seventy, but at forty, you're halfway there."

Harry and Tonto was the first film that Mazursky made entirely on location, shooting in sequence as much as possible. The cast and crew traveled across the country for nine weeks the way the character did in the script. Although this was primarily motivated by the tight budget, Mazursky actually prefers to shoot on location. He believes that the real settings add to the reality of the film and that shooting in sequence helps actors "grow with a film—get the feel of its development."

Mazursky had to return to New York for three months in 1973 to check the New York scenes of *Harry and Tonto*, which he had written from memory. After being away from it for so many years, the city looked good to him. He and his wife had adjusted to life in California, and he had even let his straight brown hair grow down to his shoulders. But he was becoming tired of California and of making movies about it. The Mazurskys decided to split their time between their house in Beverly Hills and a town house they bought in Greenwich Village. This way they could take advantage of both places—New York, which "keeps you in touch with the mob," and California, which gives you "the perpetual feeling of walking around in your underwear."

Mazursky claims that the desire to return to New York was the source of his next film, *Next Stop, Greenwich Village*: "I would literally sit down at my desk and ask, what could I write that would keep me in New York?"

The film is about Larry Lapinsky (Lenny Baker), a young man

who leaves his parents in Brooklyn to begin a life in Greenwich Village as an actor. It is also about Mazursky's friends there in the 1950s and about how he became an actor. He insists, however, that it is not the story of his youth. "I changed people around, I changed the years, I put in things I'd heard about of what happened to people I knew." Yet many details are clearly autobiographical—the Academy Award speech Larry makes to himself on the subway platform, for instance—and Mazursky has said that he wouldn't have made the film if his parents had still been alive. He has also admitted that "the boy in the movie is like me in many ways," though "he's much nicer than I was."

Mazursky is always meticulous about finding the right actors, even for minor roles. He spent six months casting *Next Stop, Greenwich Village*. He was also very careful to convey the atmosphere with correct period details: pony tails, bobby sox, old cars, old signs, old-fashioned haircuts.

Yet this funny and touching film drew mixed reviews, often for the same reasons. One critic found it "secondhand," while another said everything about it "rang a bell." Mazursky's choice of Shelley Winters for the mother was both praised and criticized, as was his choice of the late Lenny Baker as the lead. Mazursky habitually responds to criticisms, and he defended his choice of the strange-looking, gangly actor who came from Off-Broadway theater and had only minor film credits: "I really liked it that Lenny looked like some kid in the Village, not like a movie star. . . . I wanted to make the movie about people."

His next film, by contrast, got an almost unreservedly favorable reception. *An Unmarried Woman* is about thirty-seven-year-old Erica (Jill Clayburgh), an upper-middle-class wife and mother whose stockbroker husband leaves her for a younger woman after sixteen years of marriage. It is the story of her brave and successful attempt to reestablish her identity. The film was nominated for an Academy Award as best picture and won the Bodil Award of the Copenhagen Film Editors Association. Mazursky won the

National Society of Film Critics award for best screenplay and Jill Clayburgh shared the award for best actress at the Cannes Film Festival.

Mazursky spent a long time preparing this film, trying to "get inside a woman's head." He and his wife knew many women in Erica's situation, and he interviewed many more.

Before filming, he had all the women in the cast spend two weeks together doing a variety of exercises, "so they would know each other in a way that might show up on the screen." He created a history for his characters. He asked the actors to bring in their own books, records, and objects for Erica's apartment. Even the closets were filled, although their contents didn't appear on the screen. "What you see outside the frame is as important as what you see in it," he has said. He also changed the script when actresses were uncomfortable with their lines. Clayburgh contributed the bit where Erica packs up her husband's belongings and wraps them in a sheet.

As always, he kept his actors in the dark on some crucial points. For example, he didn't tell Jill Clayburgh that the woman who played the therapist Tanya in the film, in his only improvised scene, was a real psychiatrist. He also didn't tell her and Michael Murphy, who plays her husband, what would happen in the scene where he confesses to her that he has a girl friend. "I told Michael I didn't know quite what was going to happen. 'She may hit you. She may walk away.' By this time, Michael, who's a brilliant actor, was a wreck, and this fit into my design." As it turned out, Murphy bawled and Clayburgh vomited against a lamp post.

Mazursky was closely involved in the casting of this film. He spent two weeks, for instance, looking for the right actors to play Jean and Edward, an interracial couple who would appear in only two scenes and hardly speak at all. He also cast the crowd in a party scene himself, a task most directors would assign to an assistant.

His only problem with a major role was that, in the course of casting, he decided he wanted to use the British actor Alan Bates for the male lead. He had to rewrite the part to make him an Englishman who had been living in New York for about ten years.

The most serious criticism of the film was based on its difficult theme. Some critics argued that Erica's life, with her luxurious apartment and her part-time job in an art gallery, was too easy. "I deliberately did that," Mazursky answered. "I didn't want it to be a movie about a loser. . . . I wanted to show a woman who was living a pretty good life, as many are, and who'd surrendered some real parts of herself without knowing she'd done it."

Thus, he did not begrudge her in the end her romance with the charming, stable, adoring artist Saul Kaplan (Alan Bates). This character also gives Mazursky the opportunity to provide a fascinating demonstration of how an abstract painter works. Bates spent a week with Paul Jenkins, the artist whose studio and paintings are used in the film, before this scene was shot.

Although Mazursky dedicated the film in an end title to his wife, he insisted that she was not the "unmarried woman." She disagreed. "It's totally about *me*. I used to be a children's librarian, but for the past twenty years, I've been mainly at home with the children. Now I'm fifty-one and I feel the need to go back to work, to have a life of my own."

For his next film Mazursky moved away from his own generation to study the generation of the seventies. *Willie and Phil* follows three characters—two men and the woman they are both in love with—through what he sees as a decade of confusion. Some critics found the film overly sentimental, lacking the satirical bite of his other films (with its lines like "Never tell me that you love me; just love me"). Others saw it as an unsuccessful homage to François Truffaut's *Jules and Jim*, which is also about the relationships between two men and a woman. Mazursky has denied that it was a remake and said that the Truffaut film, set at

Mazursky filming *Tempest*.

the turn of the century, was only one element of his: "I am saying, in the seventies, how much it's changed . . . even though the outer form could appear to be the same."

Whatever critics said, his actors remained loyal and admiring. Margot Kidder, who played the female lead, Jeannette, said of Mazursky, "His truth meter is so precise that you can't get away with even one false moment. He demands the real you, not a battery of tricks. I've learned more from working with him than I did in twelve years of acting."

For the three weeks of rehearsal, Mazursky had the actors spend time together, often in the small Greenwich Village apartment where many of the important scenes take place. They got to know each other and, he has said, "We spent so much time there that the place got very cozy and comfortable and lived in before we ever shot a foot of film, precisely the effect I wanted."

Even after the commercial setback of *Willie and Phil*, Mazursky didn't have any trouble getting backing for his next film. Though personal, his films were familiar in style to studio executives, not dangerously avant-garde. More important, they were cheap by Hollywood standards (only *Willie and Phil* cost more than $2 million).

Mazursky is known for bringing his films in under budget. He avoids high-priced stars because he can find good actors and make them stars. He also prepares his films carefully, planning the shooting schedule and scouting locations well in advance. By the end of the pre-production period he knows what the schedule will be within a day or two and can afford to be relaxed on the set. For *Willie and Phil* he had a wall chart with the times of day and year for every interior and exterior shot.

Mazursky's next project was one he had had in mind for more than ten years—a film based loosely on Shakespeare's play *The Tempest*. "I did not feel ready for it until I finally forgot about doing it as straight Shakespeare," he has said. "Nobody will ever be able to compete in visuals with what Shakespeare does with words." The film is about Philip, a successful, fifty-year-old architect who is in the throes of a midlife crisis. He chucks it all—wife and job—and sets up as ruler of a lonely Greek island with his daughter and a charming singer (Susan Sarandon) whom he picks up in Athens. Mazursky, the successful fifty-two-year-old filmmaker, has said that "this movie's not about me, but it's always about me in the end."

Although the theme fits the Mazursky mold, *Tempest* is different from his other films. "I wanted to do something that I'd never done before," he has said. "I wanted to do a movie that would have some of the free form of Shakespeare's plays, where almost incidentally, you have a little song, a little dance, some low comedy, a little relief." The best instance of this occurs when the goatherd Kalibanos (Raul Julia) with his pipe calls up the voice of Liza Minnelli from *New York, New York* and a full orchestra. His goats leap with joy to the music.

With a budget of $13 million, *Tempest* is also on a larger scale than his other films. It was shot in Greece, and Mazursky hired a special-effects artist to produce the storm. Mazursky has said he was after the "big fish" and "you can only do that with the big movie, the hit." Unfortunately, *Tempest* has not been a hit. The general critical consensus was that it was "overblown."

Mazursky has already finished a draft of a new film. Perhaps like Philip the architect, with this one he will decide to return home again, to the smaller-scale movies that suit his themes.

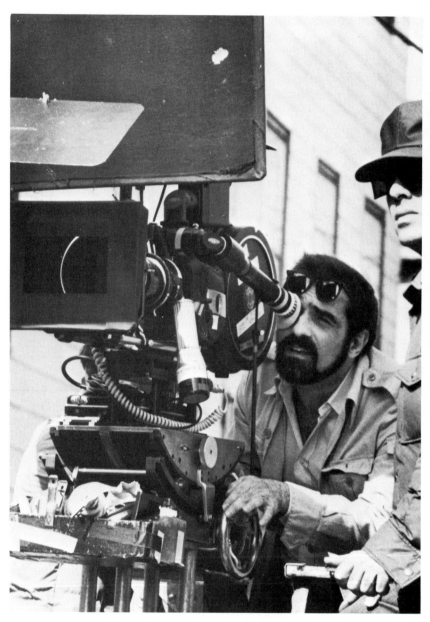

Martin Scorsese sets up a shot for *The King of Comedy*. PHOTO: Courtesy of 20th Century-Fox

Martin Scorsese

Who's That Knocking at My Door? (1967)
Boxcar Bertha (1972)
Mean Streets (1973)
Alice Doesn't Live Here Anymore (1974)
Taxi Driver (1976)
New York, New York (1977)
The Last Waltz (1978)
Raging Bull (1981)
The King of Comedy (1983)

THE SAME ADJECTIVE—"intense"—is often applied both to Martin Scorsese and to his work. This should be no surprise, for Scorsese's films are very personal. He takes characters, places, stories, and themes directly from his own life to create his films. What is perhaps surprising is that with this material he has been able to capture a public as well as a critical following.

Martin Scorsese was born on November 17, 1942, in Flushing, Queens. His parents worked in the garment industry, his father as a clothes presser, his mother as a seamstress. They had recently moved to Queens from Little Italy in Manhattan, but finances forced them to return when Marty was eight and his brother Frankie was fifteen. Scorsese grew up in a three-room tenement apartment, where his parents still live.

115

The sound and feel of the New York streets he knew so well became the sound and feel of Scorsese's films. And the undertone of violence became their undertone: "Coming home at night, it was like running an obstacle course. . . . There was always fighting going on . . . always blood in the streets. We saw fighting as the answer to most problems."

Scorsese describes his childhood as lonely; he was always an outsider. At the age of four he developed severe asthma, a condition from which he still suffers. He wasn't able to keep up with the other kids physically, and he wasn't very popular. They nicknamed him Marty Pills because of all the medication he took. Marty, unlike the guys in *Mean Streets*, didn't "hang out" much. Some of the details in that film—the fight scene in the poolroom, for instance—came to him secondhand: "I came home from school at three and sat at the kitchen table making up stories on my drawing board or watching TV or escaping to the movies . . . not being able to play ball or to fight. So I went off in the other direction, as chronicler of the group, trying to be a nice guy to have around." His poor health may also be one source of his intensity: "I'm convinced I have very little time left—physically. I just believe it. And I've got to do what's important."

Religion—Catholicism—played a big part in Scorsese's early life, and as a result, his characters are concerned with the existence of God, guilt and redemption, and humanity's ultimate end. As a boy, he wouldn't eat meat on Friday and he believed that he would go to hell if he missed Sunday mass. He entered a junior seminary and was crushed when he was expelled for bad behavior. Scorsese continued to dream of becoming "an ordinary parish priest" until he was rejected by a college divinity program and found his true vocation—film—at New York University.

Today Scorsese no longer practices Catholicism and considers himself an agnostic. But he talks about a legacy of guilt: "I've never gotten over the ritual of Catholicism." He left the Church not long after his first marriage, to a half-Jewish, half-Irish girl in

1965. "There were problems about mortal sin, certain sexual things. But what *really* did it was sitting in a church in Los Angeles and hearing a priest call the Vietnam War a holy war."

Scorsese has a very close, warm relationship with his parents, as is obvious from *Italianamerican*, the documentary he made about them in 1974. In their apartment, they talk about the old days, as Catherine Scorsese makes her spaghetti sauce. His parents also have bit parts in some of his other films.

The Scorseses are proud of their son and have always supported his career. "There were times when he was working at NYU when I used to get into a cab and bring him some food and then wait to make sure he ate it," his mother has said. His father scraped up the money for his first short films and took out student loans to support his first feature.

It was also his father who got him hooked on movies at an early age. They went to the movies together at least three times a week. Then, when Marty got home, he would draw detailed sequences from the films, frame by frame, color them in, and pull them through a cardboard movie screen. Now he draws sketches for his own films. Most of them are at least partly worked out scene by scene with all the camera angles before they are shot.

As a boy, he also staged epics on the roof of his apartment building. One he actually filmed, based on his script and storyboards, and accompanied with a tape of dialogue and music. *Vesuvius VIII*, a parody of the television series "Surfside 6," was set in ancient Rome because sheets were the only costumes available.

The films Scorsese saw while growing up provide a lodestone of images on which he can draw. He still keeps lists called "Movies I Saw This Year," which he began in childhood, and his own films are crammed with references to and even clips from his favorites. "I will always have things about movies in my movies," he has said. "I can't help it. I love movies—it's my whole life and that's it."

Asked by a film magazine what films he loved most, Scorsese almost couldn't restrain himself. He listed one hundred, some of which he's seen more than forty times, and said, "Those weren't all." The films that most influenced him, he said, are *Scorpio Rising*, *Duel in the Sun*, and the Westerns of John Ford. Elsewhere he commented on directors. "The director I feel closest to is [Samuel] Fuller, his camera movement, his aggressiveness, the emotional and physical impact of his films."

Scorsese graduated from NYU in 1964 and from its graduate school of film in 1967. He taught there while he was a graduate student and also during the two years after he got his degree. He credits NYU mainly with giving him the opportunity to use equipment and to make films. He directed five films in his time there, all of which won awards.

One of these—*Who's That Knocking at My Door?*—became his first feature. It's the story of J.R., an Italian Catholic boy who falls in love with a girl from a different world: she reads foreign magazines, lives alone, and—most important—has been raped. He can't break away from his upbringing enough to accept her when he finds this out.

This early film contains many of the basic elements of Scorsese's style. It has a loose structure and an improvisational look. The sound track is filled with rock music, and he combines a hand-held camera, zooms, and tracking movements with tight, fast editing. There are also film references: at the couple's first meeting, they discuss John Ford's *The Searchers*. Only Scorsese's characteristic violence is missing from this film.

Scorsese made the film for $35,000, most of which was raised by one of his teachers at NYU. It took two years, on and off, to shoot and another two years to find a distributor. The one they finally found took the film on the condition (which Scorsese accepted) that a sex scene be added, even though the girl in the scene appears nowhere else in the film. The reviews were respectful, but not enthusiastic.

During all this time, Scorsese took on various odd jobs in films to keep food on the table. He was an editor of news film at CBS, he made commercials in Europe, he worked on John Cassavetes's *Minnie and Moskowitz*. He also was supervising editor of the rock film *Woodstock* and accomplished the extraordinary feat of shaping more than one hundred hours of film into three.

In 1971 he went to Hollywood to edit *Medicine Ball Caravan*, another rock film. There he met Roger Corman, king of blood-and-gore exploitation films. Corman had liked *Who's That Knocking at My Door?* and asked Scorsese to direct *Boxcar Bertha*, the sequel to his *Bloody Mama*. The film is about a couple during the depression who meet their doom fighting the railroad bosses.

Corman told Scorsese that he could make the film any way he wanted so long as it had the right proportions of action, nudity, and violence and so long as he spent no more than twenty-four days on location in Kansas. Scorsese used his sharp eye for period detail and locale well and filled the film with references to action-adventure movies. It received some favorable reviews (the *New York Times* critic called it "beautifully directed"), but *Variety*'s critic wrote, "*Boxcar Bertha* is not much more than an excuse to slaughter a lot of people."

In a long conversation after the filming of *Boxcar Bertha*, John Cassavetes persuaded Scorsese not to go on with Corman but to try to return to personal filmmaking. Scorsese dug out an old script he had begun with a classmate at NYU and with unaccountable good luck met an enthusiastic novice producer at a dinner party. Suddenly he had $550,000 and twenty-seven days to make *Mean Streets*, although he could afford only six of these on location in New York. The rest was shot in Los Angeles.

The main character of the film, Charlie, is a direct outgrowth of J.R. in *Who's That Knocking at My Door?* and is played by the same actor, Harvey Keitel. Charlie is also, in some sense, Scorsese himself. He has said that he was "compelled" to make this film and that it was a "purging" for him: "The conflicts within Charlie were within me, my own feelings.

Mean Streets is the story of a would-be saint who is caught between loyalty to his girl friend Teresa and his crazed, self-destructive friend Johnny Boy (Robert De Niro) on the one side; and on the other side by his desire to rise in his gangster uncle's local racketeering organization. The Church is important to Charlie, and he knows he is a sinner, but he constantly reminds God that he is trying. He also keeps testing hell's fires by sticking his finger into a flame.

The plot meanders, its incidents revolving around Johnny Boy, who irresponsibly has defaulted on his payments to a loan shark. He doesn't even offer excuses. It turns out at last that Charlie has overestimated himself: he can't be everything to everybody. He tries to drive his friends to safety and instead heads them into a blast of gunfire.

The setting in Little Italy is straight from Scorsese's childhood. In fact, some of the scenes were shot in his parents' home. He has also said that 95 percent of the story actually happened. But the film is personal on another level, too. "When I first wrote it," he has said, "it was like an allegory for what was happening to me trying to make movies. . . . I drew from personal experiences about a guy trying to make it."

The pulsating, loud score of *Mean Streets* attests to Scorsese's lifelong passion for music. Today his traveling tape collection includes the opera *Don Giovanni*, and he keeps his radio tuned to rock 'n' roll. He carefully selected about twenty-five songs for the film, a conflicting combination of sixties rock and traditional Italian music. The feeling of potential violence is emphasized by the red lighting in the bar and the use of a hand-held camera.

The film's small budget allowed the cast only ten days of rehearsal time. "The characters and attitudes were basic to all of us," Scorsese has said. Keitel had played J.R., and Robert De Niro (Johnny Boy) comes from a background similar to Scorsese's. Other major characters were played by New Yorkers, and many of the extras were old friends of Scorsese's who just happened to be hanging around. There were only three or four improvisations on camera, but during rehearsal some improvisations were videotaped and written into the script—a technique Scorsese uses in all of his films.

Scorsese himself plays two roles in *Mean Streets*: he speaks the first line ("You don't pay for your sins in church, but in the streets"), and he is the one who pulls the trigger on Charlie and his friends as they are trying to escape.

Perhaps too disturbing for most audiences, *Mean Streets* did not do very well at the box office. The reviews, however, were adulatory. The big question remained: would Martin Scorsese be able to do it again, with other stories in other settings?

He took the challenge head on with *Alice Doesn't Live Here Anymore*, a witty film about a woman from a New Mexico suburb. Alice Hyatt (Ellen Burstyn) is set free from a stifling marriage by the death of her truck-driver husband. She and her wisecracking son hit the road for Monterey, where she hopes to fulfill her childhood dream of becoming a singer. The fact that she settles down in the end with a comfortable rancher (Kris Kristofferson) inflamed some feminist critics. But Scorsese answered that this was not intended to be a feminist film and that "Alice needs a relationship with a man. That's her character."

Nevertheless, he had hired women for key production roles and consulted them constantly about whether the emotions in the film were accurate. And one reason he gave for deciding to make the film was: "I wanted to better understand my relationships with women."

By this time Scorsese had married, had a daughter, and been divorced. He was living with the associate producer of *Alice*. That romance ended, and in 1975 he married Julia Cameron, a journalist, and had another daughter. When that marriage also ended, he married Isabella Rossellini in 1979, the daughter of

Ingrid Bergman and filmmaker Roberto Rossellini. They are now divorced.

Warner Brothers gave Scorsese a budget of $1.6 million for *Alice*. This allowed him to spend $85,000 to create a summer evening set for a flashback. In the beginning he shows Alice as a little girl who "wants to sing just as good as Alice Faye," in a scene recalling *The Wizard of Oz*. The budget also gave him time to rehearse and to improvise. The actors experimented with their lines in front of a videotape machine and sent the results to the screenwriter for approval or rewrite. Harvey Keitel, who plays Alice's psychotic lover Ben and has been in most of Scorsese's films, has talked about working with him, "Marty lets actors bring their own humanity—their eccentricities, their humor, their compassion—to a role. With Marty you have freedom, and you know something always pops up."

Although *Alice* is a film completely different in tone from *Mean Streets* (one reason he was attracted to it), it is still recognizably Scorsese's. He continued to use a hand-held camera a great deal. One reason he gave for this was that he often filmed action in very small rooms. Also, he has said, "I wanted to suggest a psychological uneasiness in the character or drop a hint of what was coming in order to make the audience feel subconsciously uneasy." He does this, for instance, before the jarringly violent scene when Ben bursts in on Alice.

The score, also, is carefully thought out. "The choice of music," Scorsese has said, "came from the characters' heads." Alice listens to songs like "Where or When" and "I've Got a Crush on You," and her son listens to rock 'n' roll.

Although reviews were mixed and some critics dismissed the film as just another cotton candy romance, it was a box office hit, and Ellen Burstyn (Alice) won an Oscar for best actress. Scorsese has been accused of selling out to Hollywood with *Alice*, but he insists that it is a highly personal film: "The feelings, the emotions, and the situations are pretty similar to things I am going through or have gone through. . . . *Alice* is from my life; it's just not blatant."

In 1974, just before filming *Alice*, Scorsese made a blatantly personal film, *Italianamerican*, the affectionate, moving documentary about his parents. It received a standing ovation when it was shown at the New York Film Festival.

Scorsese's next film was *Taxi Driver*, the story of a crazy New York City cab driver, Travis Bickle, played by Robert De Niro. Travis sees only the ugliness of the city as he drives at night—the physical and human debris. He is alienated and ready to explode with violence at anything. He assembles an arsenal of guns, exercises his body, and even gives himself a Mohawk haircut in preparation for assassinating a political candidate. When that fails, he feels compelled to rescue Iris, a twelve-year-old prostitute, from her pimp.

Another "false saint," like Charlie, Scorsese said, "the guy sets out to save people who don't want to be saved and ends up hurting them." He also said, "I know this guy Travis. I've had the feelings he has. . . . I know the feeling of rejection that Travis feels, of not being able to make relationships survive. I know . . . the feeling of really being angry."

Scorsese plays a small role in the film, a passenger who orders Travis to stop outside an apartment building where he says his wife is having an affair with a black man. He describes in brutal detail how he is going to kill her. Although Scorsese denies that he is an actor, Pauline Kael wrote in the *New Yorker* that his scene "burns a small hole in the screen."

Scorsese stayed much closer to this script than to the others, and only three or four scenes in the film are improvised. But according to the screenwriter, Paul Schrader, "Marty's not an easy person to work with. . . . One of the reasons that Marty's good is that he's headstrong and stubborn, he has a very strong view of himself. . . . Therefore, he often takes criticism as a child takes a beating, wincing at every blow."

In *Taxi Driver*, Scorsese brilliantly evokes the hot, dirty streets of a New York summer. The score, with its sense of doom, is by Bernard Herrmann, whose dissonant music is known for suggesting psychological disorder. Oddly, though, there is not one hand-held shot in the film. "The subject matter is so strong in *Taxi Driver*," Scorsese has said, "that the camera movements don't have to take over . . . but the funny thing is, no hand-held shots and the picture still looks like a documentary."

Tension builds in the film until the bloody ending, when Travis shoots Iris's pimp and all the other seedy characters around. There was much controversy over this scene, but Scorsese insists that it is necessary to provide release for the audience: "If you are going to deal with violence, it has got to be cathartic." Threatened with an X rating, however, Scorsese toned down the red of the spurting blood.

To everyone's surprise, the critical and financial success of *Taxi Driver* was even greater than that of *Alice*, and the film won top prize at the Cannes Film Festival in 1976.

One sad footnote was the role *Taxi Driver* apparently played in the attempted assassination of President Reagan in 1981. John W. Hinckley, Jr., claimed to have seen the film at least fifteen times and in many ways modeled himself on Travis Bickle— from his clothes to his diary to his obsession with "Iris." Hinckley said that he wanted to impress Jodie Foster, who played the young prostitute. He phoned and wrote her and even followed her around her college campus. After he was convicted, he said that he likes to think that he "altered her life forever."

In 1975, Martin Scorsese gave this formula for surviving in Hollywood: "If you can take on a variety of commercially appealing movies, movies you can learn from, and every once in a while sandwich in a labor of love, like *Taxi Driver*, you're doing okay." *New York, New York* was meant to be his "commercially appealing movie," a homage to the Hollywood musicals of the 1940s and early 1950s. He researched his subject painstakingly, viewing again all the more dramatic musicals of that period. United Artists gave him a budget of more than $9 million, which he spent on period sets, period costumes, and six hundred extras. He also spent $350,000 on a single production number.

Scorsese had said before he made the film, "I wanted to make a big commercial Hollywood movie, and still get my theme across." That theme is the relationship of two people who are in love but can't make it work. Francine Evans (Liza Minnelli) is a singer of popular music ("as sweet as she sings, that's how sweet she is," her manager gushes). Jimmy Doyle (Robert De Niro) is a temperamental jazz saxophonist. Her career soars, his doesn't.

There were problems with the screenplay, and Scorsese finally shot with only a story outline, using videotaped improvisations to rewrite the script. He said afterward that *New York, New York* "turned out to be one of the most personal films I've ever made." The movies of the forties remind him of his uncles in uniform.

Also, years later, he realized "that in making that film I was chronicling the painful disintegration of my own marriage." His wife, like Jimmy Doyle's, was pregnant, and thus his art, like Doyle's, was "on the line." There were also rumors of a romance between him and his star.

New York, New York was far from a success, commercially or critically. Some reviewers thought that the original genre was not interesting enough to warrant so much attention. Others didn't like the abrasive edge of the film (in one scene, for instance, Doyle strikes his pregnant wife). Musical fans couldn't have a good time. Re-released in 1981, however, the film fared much better with the critics.

While still polishing *New York*, Scorsese directed Liza Minnelli in a play called *The Act*, which was vaguely intended to be an extension of the movie. He had no theatrical experience and made some bad beginner's mistakes. The play sold out because of Minnelli's drawing power but was a critical disaster, and Scorsese was replaced as director.

Meanwhile, he had already begun working on *The Last Waltz*, which has been called the best rock film ever made. It is a documentary of the last concert given by The Band in the fall of 1976, when they shared the stage with all the great rock stars of the seventies. Scorsese outdid even his usually thorough planning. Each page of the shooting script was divided into columns for singer, lyrics, tone, lighting, and camera; everything was precisely choreographed.

During this same hectic period, he shot *American Boy*, a short documentary about his friend and business associate Steve Prince, which was never released. "I like to do documentaries while I do features," Scorsese has said, "to keep my hand in. That's when you go back to the roots."

Scorsese described his next film, *Raging Bull*, also as being close to the roots. It is the story of the rise and fall of Jake La Motta, world middleweight boxing champion of 1949. When Robert De Niro first brought La Motta's autobiography to Scorsese, he resisted. Then he began to see some of his own themes in the story of "a guy attaining something and losing everything, and then redeeming himself." The violence of this man's life—both in the ring and at home—also struck a familiar note.

Two different screenwriters worked on the script. But in the end Scorsese and De Niro, who had been talking it through for two months, went off for ten days to a Caribbean island to write it together.

Scorsese said that he wanted the film to be "real" above all else. With precision, he re-created the details of the New York Italian neighborhoods of the 1940s. He did research in gyms and boxing stadiums. "I was struck by two images," he has said, "the bloody sponges and the blood dripping from the ropes, and I used them in the film."

He deliberately cast nonprofessionals and unfamiliar actors whose style suited his and De Niro's conception of the characters. Joe Pesci, who played Jake's brother, had made only one film, which they had seen, and was working as a restaurant manager. Pesci saw Cathy Moriarty's photograph in a disco slide show and was struck by her resemblance to Vickie, Jake's wife. Scorsese tested her for three months—her only acting experience—then gave her the role. He hired fighters, trainers, and ring announcers for small parts.

The most awesome element of realism, however, was provided by Robert De Niro. His role spanned La Motta's life from the trim young fighter of the 1940s and 1950s to the obese, pathetic nightclub personality of the 1960s. In addition to working out in a gym with La Motta every day for a year, De Niro spent a four-month break in the filming gaining fifty-five pounds.

Scorsese shot *Raging Bull* in black and white. He wanted to recall viewers' memories of boxing in the forties and fifties, which are mainly from black-and-white films. Scorsese is also very concerned about the problem of color film fading. The color film that most filmmakers use is unstable. In as little as ten years, the blues and yellows begin to disappear, leaving only a pinkish purple. For the past few years Scorsese has led a campaign to force Eastman Kodak and the studios to do something about this.

Raging Bull was controversial. Some critics called it a masterful achievement, while others faulted it for lacking motivation. Nevertheless, it won two Academy Awards—for best actor and best editing—and was nominated for six others, including best director.

Scorsese's newest film, *The King of Comedy*, opened to mixed reviews. It is the story of an aspiring comic, Rupert Pupkin (Robert De Niro) who, in an attempt to get his big break on TV, kidnaps his idol, a talk show host played by Jerry Lewis. Scorsese has said of him: "Rupert's an extension of me inasmuch as he'd do *anything* to get what he wanted. . . . He was to comics as I was to the movies. . . . Rupert reminds me of the hunger I had in the sixties." He has also said that the film is about "a person's right to be by himself, within himself," something Scorsese

Scorsese discusses a scene in *The King of Comedy* with Robert De Niro.
PHOTO: Courtesy of 20th Century-Fox

understands after years of being a celebrity in the film industry.

With this film, as with his others, Martin Scorsese seems to be aiming for a personal goal. "I want to communicate on the basic human level," he once said, "sad, funny, violent, painful. I don't want to do movies unless they further me not only as a filmmaker but as a person."

Steven Spielberg directing *E.T.*

Steven Spielberg

The Sugarland Express (1974)
Jaws (1975)
Close Encounters of the Third Kind (1977)
1941 (1979)
Raiders of the Lost Ark (1981)
Poltergeist (1982, executive producer)
E.T. The Extra-Terrestrial (1982)

STEVEN SPIELBERG, at the age of thirty-five, is the director of four of the top-grossing movies of all time. He has been described as an instinctive movie craftsman and, like other personal directors in Hollywood, is involved in his films from their conception through their release. He has also been described as a "popcorn" director, which doesn't embarrass him at all. "I think that popular movies that are well made are an indication that you're not working in a vacuum," he has said, and "I never want to stop entertaining."

Spielberg started entertaining as a child. He was born in Cincinnati on December 18, 1947, and was uprooted several times as his father, a computer engineer, took jobs at different electronics firms in New Jersey, Arizona, and finally California (when Steven was seventeen). He has said that he was a "wimp" as a child, a skinny kid with big ears, who couldn't play sports and couldn't

131

fix cars. "I was a loner and very lonely. I was the only Jewish kid in school, and I was very shy and uncertain." It was not until high school that he found fellow spirits—in the theater arts program. "That's when I realized there were options besides being a jock or a wimp."

At home he applied his theatrical gifts to torturing his three younger sisters. He would tell them bedtime horror stories, then after they were asleep, go to their window with a flashlight and call, "I am the moo-oo-oo-oon."

Spielberg's mother was a former concert pianist, and she arranged music lessons for him at an early age. He now considers music his "second love" and has a vast collection of sound track recordings. His parents were very strict about television and movies, however. On TV he saw only Soupy Sales, Sid Caesar, and "The Honeymooners." Although he occasionally sneaked out to movies like *I Was a Teenage Werewolf*, he usually went with his parents to general audience features or Disney cartoons. It wasn't until he was a professional filmmaker that he began to see the great classics. He still does not consider himself a film scholar.

Spielberg became involved in films more from doing than from seeing. The Spielbergs often went backpacking and camping in the woods together, and he was in charge of the family's home movies. "I began actually to stage the camping trips and later cut the bad footage out," he has said. Spielberg's first films were *Father Chopping Wood*, *Mother Digging Latrine*, *Young Sister Removing Fishhook From Right Eye*, and *Bear in the Bushes*. "Sometimes I would just have fun and shoot two frames of this and three frames of that and ten frames of something else, and it got to the point where the documentaries were more surrealistic than factual."

Soon he began making 8-millimeter silent movies. He wrote the scripts, drew the storyboards for hours alone in his room, and used neighborhood kids in the cast. Most of these were horror films, a rebellion against his parents' strictness, and involved buckets of blood. He would charge 25¢ admission to cover the costs.

At thirteen, Spielberg earned a Boy Scout merit badge in photography with a three-minute Western he made called *The Last Gun*. When he showed the film to the troop, "I got whoops and screams and applause and everything else that made me want it more and more." Other Westerns and war films followed, growing more technically sophisticated. At fifteen, Spielberg won first prize in an amateur film festival for a fifteen-minute war picture called *Escape to Nowhere*.

At sixteen, he wrote, directed, shot, and edited a two-and-a-half-hour 8-millimeter sound feature called *Firelight*. Like his later film, *Close Encounters of the Third Kind*, it is about a team of scientists investigating mysterious lights in the sky. His father bankrolled about $300 of the $500 budget. The rest Steven earned by whitewashing citrus trees for 75¢ apiece. He made it all back and cleared $50 in a one-night showing at a rented theater.

When the group assembled to see the movie, Spielberg said, "I knew what I wanted. . . . I wanted Hollywood." But his grades were too low for him to get into any college with a film program. He went to California State at Long Beach, which didn't even have a film history course ("just to be close to Hollywood") and nominally majored in English. What he actually did was make films and go constantly to movie theaters and student film festivals. He also claims that for three months he dressed up in a suit and, carrying a briefcase, walked unnoticed into an empty office on the Universal lot, where he could watch directors and editors at work.

During college he made many short 16-millimeter films, which he has described as "very esoteric." His break came when a young would-be producer arranged to get him $10,000 to make a twenty-four-minute film called *Amblin'*, about a boy and a girl who meet in the Mojave Desert and hitchhike together to the Pacific Ocean. It won awards at film festivals in Atlanta and Venice and so impressed the president of Universal's television division that he gave Spielberg a seven-year contract.

Yet Spielberg has called the film a "Pepsi commercial" and said that it "was a conscious effort to break into the business and become successful by proving to people I could move a camera and compose nicely and deal with lighting and performances. The only challenge that's close to my heart about *Amblin'* is I was able to tell a story about a boy and a girl with no dialogue. That was something I set out to do before I found out I couldn't afford sound even if I wanted it."

At the age of twenty-one, Steven Spielberg began his career as a television director by directing a show starring Joan Crawford. He made ten episodes in all for series that included "Marcus Welby," "The Psychiatrists," and "Columbo." He also made three television movies before he went on to direct feature films. He has said that he took his TV work seriously, worrying about composition and aspect ratios on every shot: "I considered each show a mini-feature. . . . I refused to conform to . . . the television formula of closeup, two-shot, over-the-shoulder, and master shot."

Spielberg doesn't regret his television experience at all. "Television has taught me to imagine the finished product," he has said, "and then just before shooting retrace my thoughts and follow that imaginary blueprint . . . because you're making an hour show in six days. You better know line for line, shot for shot exactly what you're doing."

His care on *Duel*, a television movie based on a short story, paid off. *Duel* is the story of a mild-mannered traveling salesman whose red Plymouth Valiant is pursued by a gasoline truck with an unseen driver intent on destroying him. This is a theme that reappears in Spielberg's work: the ordinary man who rises to heroism when he has to confront a menacing force.

Duel was shot in sixteen days for $425,000, and Spielberg has said that it was a much greater challenge than the big-budget *Jaws*: "Trying to create that kind of fear out of a truck is a lot harder than the established fear of a man-eating fish underwater." The film was released in theaters in Europe, where it earned Universal $9 million and won several prestigious awards.

After *Duel*, Spielberg got many feature film offers, including the chance to direct *White Lightning*, a Burt Reynolds picture. He had worked on it for two and a half months before he realized that he "didn't want to start my career as a hardhat journeyman director. I wanted to do something that was a little more personal." He took off a year and wrote a twenty-page treatment for *Sugarland Express*. It was based on a newspaper story about a young criminal and his wife. They kidnapped a policeman and drove across Texas with him in search of their baby, who was taken away by the welfare department.

Spielberg went back to television work and then, two years later, hired two writers to make his treatment into a screenplay, which Richard Zanuck and David Brown produced for Universal. Spielberg has said that the film "made an important statement about the Great American Dream Machine that can transform two innocent people into celebrities." Although some reviewers doubted whether it was saying that—or anything else—it was, nevertheless, a critical success. The performances were praised (Goldie Hawn's Lou Jean was said to be the best role of her career); the choreography of the two hundred and fifty cars that followed the fugitives was said to be masterly; and the screenplay won an award at Cannes. Pauline Kael wrote in the *New Yorker*: "In terms of the pleasure that technical assurance gives an audience, this film is one of the most phenomenal debut films in the history of movies."

Sugarland Express only just broke even at the box office. Its producers were impressed enough with Spielberg, however, that when he asked to direct a movie based on a novel he had picked up in their office, they agreed. That novel was *Jaws*. This is the story of a summer beach community that is terrorized by the appearance near shore of a man-eating shark. It is also about the greedy local authorities who try to hide the truth to save the tourist trade.

In the last part, which attracted Spielberg, three men who have little in common—a tough old sea dog (Robert Shaw), a wealthy ichthyologist (Richard Dreyfuss), and the town's New York–bred police chief (Roy Scheider)—go out in a boat together to hunt the shark. Only two return, but they kill the shark.

The shark itself doesn't appear until more than an hour into the film. Instead, low, growling chords play and the camera zigzags underwater to indicate its presence. Spielberg deliberately used this device, which he insisted on as soon as he read the manuscript, to build tension and suspense.

Jaws was a very difficult film to make, and in the course of production, the budget doubled to $8 million. The most persistent problems were the unpredictable weather and the unreliable mechanical sharks, all nicknamed Bruce, after Spielberg's lawyer. But there were others. Because of an impending actors' strike, Spielberg was given only three and a half months to prepare, instead of the year he said he needed. He usually sketches every shot of his films in stick figures, from which an artist does the detailed drawings of the storyboards. For *Jaws*, he could do this only for the last part. The rest was planned a week or a day in advance, or even on the set. "I did not begin *Jaws* with a visual conception of the finished product—as I did *Sugarland*," he has said. There was also no time for rehearsing the actors. The cast wasn't even together when shooting began, and some of the small parts were cast as they came up.

The screenplay was another major problem. There were six drafts and five writers, including Spielberg, and the result was "a script I didn't care for and had to improvise my way through." The actors, he has said, "contributed more to their dialogue than any of the writers." They went through each day's dialogue at Spielberg's house the evening before. A writer would be there to take down the improvisations that worked well.

Spielberg has always had a good rapport with his actors, perhaps because he acted in high-school plays and took two years of acting classes. Richard Dreyfuss, who starred in both *Jaws* and *Close Encounters of the Third Kind*, has said that Spielberg is a good director to work with "because, unlike some directors, he actually *knows* what he wants." Dreyfuss has also said, "Steve's not what you would call an actor's director in the classical sense. But he's relaxed and open in the way he communicates what he wants, and he helps you to get there."

"The most important thing about a film," Spielberg has said, "is the story." But he likes to give actors enough freedom so that "they can show me things that I didn't come prepared to show them." There are only two things that he is a tyrant about— "where to put the camera and where to make the splice." He is also a perfectionist, who will shoot scenes over and over until they satisfy him. And he never considers a film finished until he has previewed it before a real audience. Three weeks before *Jaws* was to open, he discovered at a preview that two of what were supposed to be the scariest moments didn't work as well as they should have: when a dead man's head pops out of a hole in a sunken boat's hull and when the shark first leaps out of the water. He edited again and used his own money to shoot new underwater footage in a swimming pool.

Most critics reviewed *Jaws* as a well-crafted scare movie, but nothing more. Spielberg himself has said of it, "Lots of filmmakers want to do something important. There's great validity in wanting to do something that enriches someone else's life. But there's also nothing wrong with a fast-food movie if it's done with skill and affection and honesty. And *Jaws* was that kind of picture."

The film grossed $400 million, more than any other film at

that time, and the Hollywood studios were impressed. When Spielberg turned down the opportunity to direct the sequel for Universal, Columbia executives told him he could make whatever movie he wanted at whatever cost. He chose *Close Encounters of the Third Kind*, which he had conceived before *Jaws*.

Spielberg has said that the film about contact with extraterrestrials was "a personal statement out of my own head." He related it to his childhood, when he would look up into the clear Arizona skies through his homemade reflecting telescope. He also clearly remembered his father, a science fiction buff, waking him up in the middle of the night and driving him to a far-off field to see a spectacular meteor shower.

Spielberg spent a year doing research, reading about UFOs, and also interviewing people who had had extraordinary experiences. In fact, the appearance of the chief alien, designed by Carlo Rambaldi (who also designed E.T.), was based on people's reports.

He then wrote the screenplay himself. He doesn't consider himself a writer and prefers to collaborate with others, but in the case of *Close Encounters*, he has said, "I couldn't find anybody who would write it the way I wanted" (as a combination adventure story and personal story).

Close Encounters is the story of Roy Neary (Richard Dreyfuss), an electrical worker from Muncie, Indiana, who is seared by a blinding light and experiences strange phenomena while driving his truck one night. He becomes obsessed by the vision of a mountain, which he sculpts out of shaving cream and food. When he starts to build a model out of soil he has shoveled into the living room, his family finally abandons him. It is also the story of Jillian Guiler (Melinda Dillon), similarly obsessed, whose three-year-old son was spirited away. Both, along with other ordinary people, are drawn to Devils Tower in Wyoming, where a team of scientists is calling a spaceship with a five-note musical greeting. Their awesome encounter fills the last forty minutes of the film.

Close Encounters took two years to make, including five months of shooting. For this film, Spielberg planned every scene in detail on storyboards, producing more than fifteen hundred drawings. He has said that this preparation enhances rather than restricts his spontaneity. "I'm almost at my most improvisatory when I've planned most thoroughly, when my storyboards are in continuity."

There were countless headaches in this film also, and the budget escalated from $12 million to $18 million in the course of filming. The locations ranged from California to India, but most of it had to be shot in a huge World War II air force hangar outside Mobile, Alabama, which is six times larger than any sound stage. There were 350 special effects, engineered by a crew of more than forty animators, model makers, matte artists, optical-effects specialists, and electronics engineers. Spielberg designed and directed the special effects himself, overseeing all the photography and every element that went into a final shot. He even drilled the window holes in part of the mothership.

Since Spielberg was determined to surprise audiences with these special effects, he kept tight security on the shooting site. No one could get past the guards without an identification badge, and everyone working on the film had to take a vow of silence.

The cast included the French filmmaker François Truffaut, as the gurulike head scientist. Although he had never before acted in a film other than his own, Truffaut was working on a book called *The Actor*, and he wanted the experience of being directed. He said later that he was pleasantly surprised at the performance that Spielberg coaxed out of him.

Spielberg spent more than a year editing *Close Encounters*. Editing is the part of filmmaking that he enjoys the most, does best, and considers "the most creative part of filmmaking." The editors he works with are "just sort of completing my vision. I'm stopping the moviola on a signal frame and saying, 'Mark here.'"

Close Encounters, with its optimistic vision of extraterrestrial contact as opposed to the standard attack from outer space, got mainly enthusiastic reviews, and Spielberg was nominated for an Academy Award as best director. The major criticism was that the center part of the film was weak. Taking this to heart, Spielberg asked the studio for $1 million to make a "Special Edition" of the film, which was released in 1980. He tightened the middle and changed the ending, so that the audience gets to see the inside of the spaceship.

What followed his two blockbusters (*Close Encounters* made $250 million), was Spielberg's only total disaster, both critical and commercial. His *1941* is a comedy, starring the late actor John Belushi, about the panic that hit California after Pearl Harbor was bombed, when the citizens of Los Angeles thought they would be the next target. The film took two hectic and difficult years to make and cost $30 million.

"I had always wanted to try a visual comedy," Spielberg has said, "but with enough adventure and action where I felt that I'd be sort of in my own element and not out in the cold." He also enjoyed the studio shooting. Much of the budget had gone into building a set of the Los Angeles of forty years ago. "There was a real sense of the old tinseltown on a Hollywood sound stage."

He admitted, however, that "comedy is not my forte," and, unfortunately the critics agreed that the film was just not funny.

Analyzing his mistakes later, Spielberg has said, "Until then I thought I was immune to failure. But I couldn't come down from the power high of making big films on large canvases. I threw everything in, and it killed the soup: *1941* was my encounter with economic reality." He learned his lesson well. After three films that went substantially over budget, Spielberg made three films that were not only on budget but ahead of schedule.

The first of these, *Raiders of the Lost Ark*, was a collaboration with George Lucas, who had been a friend for eleven years. The film, a nonstop adventure that recalls the movie serials of the thirties and forties, was Lucas's idea. He and Spielberg both contributed to the writing of Lawrence Kasden's screenplay, beginning with five nine-hour days of hammering out the story together.

Set in 1936, it is about an adventurous professor of archaeology, Indiana Jones (played by Harrison Ford, who was Han Solo in *Star Wars*). He is sent by U.S. Intelligence in search of the lost Ark of the Covenant, a chest containing the original tablets of the Ten Commandments and with them the power of God. It is a race between him and Hitler's archaeologists. And the action never stops, whether Jones is risking his life in a daredevil truck chase or in a room filled with eight thousand snakes.

The film was shot in four countries on three continents and had forty optical effects, but Spielberg ran a tight ship. About 80 percent of *Raiders* was on storyboards; Spielberg had made 2,700 sketches of the scenes before shooting. He did an average of four takes per shot, as compared with twenty in the film *1941*. There was also less improvisation, he said, because he had a better script than ever before. He decided to make "a real good B-plus film. I decided not to shoot for a masterpiece but to make a good movie that told George's story very well."

As for whose film it is, that is a close question. Spielberg has said, "I was making this movie for my friend George, for his company and for his idea. I just didn't feel that it was right to impose a lot of my own expressionism into George's style." What he contributed to the film was "more humor than it would otherwise have had." He "substituted humor and invention," he later said, "for time-consuming technique and additional angles."

Spielberg said he needed *Raiders* "to exorcise myself from a kind of rut I was falling into—where I wouldn't walk away from a shot until it was 100 percent of what I intended." The film, which grossed $310 million, opened to near unanimous raves, although Stuart Byron in a dissenting review in the *Village Voice* pointed out that "even its proponents agree it is nothing but superior entertainment."

The next two Spielberg films, *Poltergeist* and *E.T. The Extra-Terrestrial*, were very much his own, although his actual title on *Poltergeist* was executive producer (Tobe Hooper was the director). Spielberg had been an executive producer of three previous films—*I Wanna Hold Your Hand, Used Cars,* and *Continental Divide*—but his personal involvement in these was small. For *Poltergeist* he collaborated on the screenplay, which was based on his original story, did the storyboards, chose the cast and locations, was on the set almost every day, and supervised the final editing.

The film, which has over a hundred optical effects, is about an ordinary suburban couple whose house is haunted by ghosts. They fly out of the TV set one night and kidnap five-year-old Carol Anne. The parents finally get her back with the help of Tangina, a psychic. Spielberg has said that the film "reflects a lot of the fears I had at night—scary shadows that could simply be bunched-up clothes or a shadow like Godzilla cast by the hall light." Reviewers generally recommended it as an entertaining thriller.

Poltergeist and *E.T.*, Spielberg's next film released a few weeks later, showed off a new side of him, which led Vincent Canby to call him "the best director of children now working in American movies." He enjoys working with children, and Robert Mac-Naughton, who plays the older brother in *E.T.*, has said that he is good at "talking to kids on their own level." Spielberg now hopes that he will be taken seriously as a director of actors. Only one of his actors (Melinda Dillon in *Close Encounters*) was ever nominated for an Academy Award.

E.T. was a great step in the direction of personal filmmaking

Spielberg and Henry Thomas on location with *E.T.*

for Spielberg. It is based on his own story about an extraterrestrial being who is accidentally left on earth by his fellow scientists, who are collecting samples to take back to their own planet. He is befriended until they return by a little boy (Elliott), who is lonely after his parents' recent divorce and doesn't have many friends at school. Spielberg's own parents separated when he was a teenager, right after they moved to California. "Divorce," he has said, "was the first scary word I remember hearing." In *E.T.*, "I'm reacting to a situation in my life. When my father left, I went from tormentor to protector with my family. I'd never assumed responsibility for anything except making my home movies. . . . I had become the man of the house." He has also said that Elliott is "not me but he's the closest thing to my experiences in life, growing up in suburbia."

E.T. marked a change in Spielberg's working style. "It's the most emotionally complicated film I've ever made and the least technically complicated," he has said. As a result, for the first time he shot without the aid of storyboards. "Using the script is the best storyboard I had, and everything else from that would be the ideas I would get from blocking a scene, looking at a set. I wasn't thinking five shots ahead. . . . I was thinking to perhaps only the next shot, but it's been better for this movie, which has so much emotion in it."

The reviews of the film were ecstatic and it set box office records, topping even *Star Wars*. There also are fifty merchandise licensing deals tied to it for everything from E.T. pajamas to E.T. bubble gum, which are expected to gross another $1 billion.

E.T. has also affected Spielberg's personal life. In early 1980 his four-year romance with the actress Amy Irving unexpectedly ended for reasons neither will discuss. Since then, Spielberg has dated a number of women, but he now seems to have settled in with Kathleen Carey, who works in the record business. After making *E.T.*, he has said, "I have this deep yearning now to become a father."

For the future, professionally, he has talked about sequels to *Close Encounters* and *E.T.* and a film he has called his *Annie Hall*—a loose remake of a 1943 love-triangle story called *A Guy Named Joe*. In January 1983 he also began filming a sequel to *Raiders*. Spielberg used to say that he didn't want his own studio. ("I have enough trouble directing movies. I don't want to be an emperor of high finance.") But recently he talked about forming a company that would be "like a children's crusade of filmmakers. The only way you can get into this company is if you haven't made a film before."

Even so, it is unlikely that Steven Spielberg will move far away from the camera. For him, filmmaking itself will always be paramount. He has described himself as a "hardworking drone. I enjoy making the movies: getting up early, having to struggle and fight the weather and fight egos and all the things that are always plotting against the completion of a project. I enjoy rolling up my sleeves and getting into it."

Blacks and Women in Hollywood

IF IT IS EXTREMELY hard to become a Hollywood director, it is ten times harder for blacks and women. For them, it is not so much a question of making personal films as of making films at all. The explanation is simple: money. "Filmmaking," Charlton Heston once said, "is the only art form where the artist can't afford his own materials." The money today is in the hands of the white male executives of the major studios.

Strangely, both blacks and women have a long history in filmmaking. An independent black film industry began in the 1920s, producing films by, about, and for blacks. They were made on tiny budgets and shown in the segregated black theaters of the South and the ghetto theaters of the North. Some of them dealt with issues of color and caste, illegitimate children, and historical events; others just mimicked white movies.

Most of the more than one hundred black film companies lasted only long enough to make a few films. The depression, the coming of sound, and the few all-black Hollywood productions finally wiped out all but one. Oscar Micheaux, called the dean of black filmmakers, continued to make films until his death in 1957. He was the producer, director, writer, editor, business manager, and promoter of about fifteen features.

Not until the late 1960s and the early 1970s did black film

directors become active again. In 1969, *Cotton Comes to Harlem* became the first commercially successful film by a black director. Ossie Davis, the actor and stage director, had financed the wild detective comedy independently. When it made $7 million, Hollywood began to sense a lucrative "new" black market.

In 1971, Melvin Van Peebles wrote, directed, produced, scored, and starred in an even more profitable movie—*Sweet Sweetback's Baadasssss Song*. Filled with coarse, realistic street language, it was the story of the radicalization of a black man. Now the studios jumped on the bandwagon with *Shaft*, *Blacula*, *Superfly*, and others. At the peak, in 1973, there were more than one hundred films aimed at the black audience.

While *Sweetback* sprang from an authentic black sensibility, many of the other new "black" films were just standard action scripts with black actors plugged in. They had weak plots, poor craftsmanship, and offensive amounts of violence and sex. They were made quickly and cheaply (for $500,000 to $800,000), but they grossed millions. Unfortunately, although they provided jobs for black writers, directors, actors, and technicians, most of the profits went to the whites who financed, produced, and distributed them.

Black critics and the black community began to object almost immediately to the aesthetic and social values of these so-called blaxploitation films, which glorified the drug culture and the lives of pimps and prostitutes. By 1975, partly because of this pressure but also because of the rising cost of making movies and the failure of *The Wiz*, the $30 million all-black film, these films had almost disappeared. The studios concluded that they didn't need black films to attract black audiences.

Today Sidney Poitier and Michael Schultz are the only black directors who work regularly on black and nonblack films, and neither is considered to have a strong authorial voice. Poitier directed *Buck and the Preacher*, *A Warm December*, *Uptown Saturday Night*, *Let's Do It Again*, *Stir Crazy*, and *Hanky*

Panky. Schultz directed *Cooley High*, *Which Way Is Up?*, *Carwash*, *Greased Lightning*, *Sergeant Pepper's Lonely Hearts Club Band*, and *Carbon Copy*.

Women, too, were active filmmakers in the era of silent film. There were more women directors in Hollywood during the 1910s and 1920s than in any period since. Approximately twenty-six women directors were working for small independent film companies, and women were involved in every aspect of filmmaking. But with the coming of sound and the increased cost of making films, these companies were wiped out by the major studios, and the number of women directors decreased sharply.

Two survivors were Dorothy Arzner and Ida Lupino. Arzner directed seventeen films between 1927 and 1943 and was one of the top ten Hollywood directors in the 1930s. Lupino made eight films through her own production company between 1949 and 1954.

It was not until the late 1960s, however, with the increased use of 16-millimeter film, that women began to appear again as producers, directors, writers, editors, and cinematographers. They began to slip into the documentary field, where the budgets were small.

Studio executives over the years have given numerous excuses for the absence of female directors, even from television, where many male directors get their training. Women don't have the technical skills, the executives claim; they can't control male crews; they don't have the physical stamina; they are stubborn and inflexible; they make messagey films.

The first woman to overcome these prejudices in the 1970s was Elaine May, who had already proved herself salable as a comedian. She directed *A New Leaf* and *The Heartbreak Kid*. Then *Mikey* and *Nicky*, which she brought in late and over budget after two agonizing years of editing, was a critical and financial disaster. This experience not only drove her from filmmaking, but also hurt the prospects of other female directors.

Several women have had a shot at Hollywood since then, but they have yet to follow up on it: Lee Grant (*Tell Me a Riddle*), Joan Tewkesbury (*Old Boyfriends*), Jane Wagner (*Moment to Moment*), Anne Bancroft (*Fatso*), and Joan Darling (*First Love*). Claudia Weill, whose independent feature *Girl Friends* was hailed at Cannes and was bought for distribution by Warner Brothers, then got $7 million to direct *It's My Turn*.

Joan Micklin Silver, however, is the only woman who has had real critical and financial success directing features in the 1970s. Her three films are *Hester Street*, *Between the Lines*, and *Chilly Scenes of Winter*.

Both blacks and women are much better represented in the independent film movement than in Hollywood. Blacks still have less access to television screenings, art houses, and museums, but the number of women independents is about equal to the number of men. Claudia Weill, however, does not see the answer here. She said she could never again make a film financed primarily by grants and loans: "I couldn't ask those kinds of favors again of my friends, to work for so little and on deferrals. . . . If, in fact, you want to make features, you pretty much—after making one like that—are forced to work within the system, because there's no middle territory."

Perhaps, then, the best hope for the future lies in two other directions—with the increasing number of women in the management of the studios, and with the new video technologies, which should provide more opportunities for all filmmakers.

Selected Bibliography

The information in this book came from many sources: general books on American film in the 1970s, books about individual filmmakers, and hundreds of articles in newspapers, general-interest magazines, and specialized film magazines. Listed below are books on film in general. Then, by filmmaker, are books about each and a selection of the pertinent magazine and newspaper articles.

GENERAL BOOKS

GELMIS, JOSEPH. *The Film Director as Superstar*. New York: Doubleday, 1970.

JACOBS, DIANE. *Hollywood Renaissance*. New York: Dell (Delta), 1980.

MONACO, JAMES. *American Film Now: The People, The Power, The Money, The Movies*. New York: New American Library, 1979.

MYLES, LYNDA, and MICHAEL PYE. *The Movies Brats: How the Film Generation Took Over Hollywood*. New York: Holt, Rinehart & Winston, 1979.

WOODY ALLEN

BOOKS

GUTHRIE, LEE. *Woody Allen: A Biography*. New York: Drake, 1978.

HIRSCH, FOSTER. *Love, Sex, Death, and the Meaning of Life: Woody Allen's Comedy*. New York: McGraw-Hill, 1981.

JACOBS, DIANE. . . . *but we need the eggs: The Magic of Woody Allen*. New York: St. Martin's, 1982.

LAX, ERIC. *On Being Funny: Woody Allen and Comedy*. New York: Charterhouse, 1975.

YACOWAR, MAURICE. *Loser Take All: The Comic Art of Woody Allen*. New York: Frederick Ungar, 1979.

ARTICLES

GITTELSON, NATALIE. "The Maturing of Woody Allen." *New York Times Magazine*, April 22, 1979.

HALBERSTADT, IRA. "Scenes from a Mind." *Take One*, November 1978.

KROLL, JACK. "Woody." *Newsweek*, April 24, 1978.

RICH, FRANK. "An Interview with Woody Allen." *Time*, April 30, 1979.

SCHICKEL, RICHARD. "The Basic Woody Allen Joke." *New York Times Magazine*, April 24, 1978.

ROBERT ALTMAN

BOOK

KASS, JUDITH M. *Robert Altman: American Innovator*. New York: Popular Library, 1978.

ARTICLES

ALTMAN, ROBERT. "Interview." *Playboy*, August 1976.

CUTTS, JOHN. "M-A-S-H, McCloud, and McCabe: An Interview with Robert Altman." *Films and Filming*, November 1971.

GRIGSBY, WAYNE. "Robert Altman: A Young Turk at 54." *Maclean's*, April 23, 1979.

GROSS, LARRY. "An Interview with Robert Altman on the Set of 'Nashville.'" *Millimeter*, February 1975.

HARMETZ, ALJEAN. "The 15th Man Who Was Asked to Direct 'M*A*S*H' (and Did) Makes a Peculiar Western." *New York Times Magazine*, June 20, 1971.

MEL BROOKS

BOOKS

ADLER, BILL, and JEFFREY FEINMAN. *Mel Brooks: The Irreverent Funnyman*. Chicago: Playboy Press, 1976.

HOLTZMAN, WILLIAM. *Seesaw: A Dual Biography of Anne Bancroft and Mel Brooks*. New York: Doubleday, 1979.

YACOWAR, MAURICE. *In Method Madness: The Comic Art of Mel Brooks*. New York: St. Martin's, 1981.

ARTICLES

BROOKS, MEL. "Interview." *Playboy*, February 1975.

RIVLIN, ROBERT. "Comedy Director: Interview with Mel Brooks." *Millimeter*, October 1977.

RIVLIN, ROBERT. "Mel Brooks on 'High Anxiety.'" *Millimeter*, December 1977.

TYNAN, KENNETH. "Frolics and Detours of a Short Hebrew Man." *New Yorker*, October 30, 1978.

ZIMMERMAN, PAUL D. "Mad, Mad Mel Brooks." *Newsweek*, February 17, 1975.

FRANCIS COPPOLA

BOOKS

COPPOLA, ELEANOR. *Notes*. New York: Pocket Books, 1979.

JOHNSON, ROBERT K. *Francis Ford Coppola*. Boston: Twyane, 1978.

ARTICLES

BRAUDY, SUSAN. "Francis Ford Coppola: A Profile." *Atlantic*, August, 1976.

DE PALMA, BRIAN. "The Making of 'The Conversation.'" *Filmmakers Newsletter*, May 1974.

FARBER, STEPHEN. "Coppola and 'The Godfather.'" *Sight and Sound*, Autumn 1972.

HALLER, SCOT. "Francis Coppola's Biggest Gamble." *Saturday Review*, July 1981.

ROSS, LILLIAN. "Some Figures on a Fantasy." *New Yorker*, November 8, 1982.

BRIAN DE PALMA

ARTICLES

AMERICAN FILM INSTITUTE. "Brian De Palma: An AFI Seminar on His Work," part 1, no. 43 (April 4, 1973). Beverly Hills, 1977.

BARTHOLOMEW, D. "De Palma of the Paradise." *Cinefantastique*, vol. 4, no. 2 (1975).

DE PALMA, BRIAN. "Brian De Palma: A Day in the Life." *Esquire*, October 1980.

DUNNING, JENNIFER. "Brian De Palma: 'I Operate on the Principle of Escalating Terror.'" *New York Times*, April 23, 1978.

KAKUTANI, MICHIKO. "De Palma: 'I'm Much More of a Romantic Than Hitchcock.' " *New York Times*, July 19, 1981.

GEORGE LUCAS

ARTICLES

FARBER, STEPHEN. "George Lucas: The Skinky Kid Hits the Big Time." *Film Quarterly,* Spring 1974.

HARMETZ, ALJEAN. "The Saga beyond 'Star Wars.'" *New York Times,* May 15, 1980.

LUCAS, GEORGE, interviewed by Mitch Tuchman and Anne Thompson. "I'm the Boss." *Film Comment,* July–August 1981.

O'QUINN, KERRY. "The George Lucas Saga," Chapters 1 and 2. *Starlog,* July and August, 1981.

SHERMAN, STRATFORD P. "The Empire Pays Off." *Fortune,* October 6, 1980.

PAUL MAZURSKY

ARTICLES

AMERICAN FILM INSTITUTE. "Paul Mazursky." *Dialogue on Film,* November, 1974.

APPELBAUM, RALPH. "Experience and Expression: Paul Mazursky." *Films and Filming,* August 1978.

GREENFIELD, JEFF. "Paul Mazursky in Wonderland." *Life,* September 4, 1970.

HALLER, SCOT. "Happily Married Man Who Examines the Shaky State of Marriage." *Horizon,* May 1978.

MONACO, JAMES. "Paul Mazursky and *Willie and Phil." American Film,* July – August 1980.

MARTIN SCORSESE

BOOK

KELLY, MARY PAT. *Martin Scorsese: The First Decade*. Pleasantville, N.Y.: Redgrave, 1980.

ARTICLES

AMERICAN FILM INSTITUTE. "Martin Scorsese." *Dialogue on Film*, April 1975.

FLATLEY, GUY. "Martin Scorsese's Gamble." *New York Times Magazine*, February 8, 1976.

HOWARD, STEVE. "The Making of 'Alice Doesn't Live Here Anymore': An Interview with Director Martin Scorsese." *Filmmakers Newsletter*, March 1975.

ROSEN, MARJORIE. "The New Hollywood: Martin Scorsese." *Film Comment*, March–April 1975.

WEINER, THOMAS. "Martin Scorsese Fights Back." *American Film*, November 1980.

STEVEN SPIELBERG

ARTICLES

AMERICAN FILM INSTITUTE. "Steven Spielberg: An AFI Seminar on His Work," part 1, nos. 170–71 (November 14, 1973; November 26, 1975). Beverly Hills, 1977.

CORLISS, RICHARD. "Steve's Summer Magic." *Time*, May 31, 1982.

JANOS, LEO. "Steven Spielberg: L'Enfant Directeur." *Cosmopolitan*, June 1980.

SWIRES, STEVE. "Filming the Fantastic: Steven Spielberg." *Starlog*, October 1978.

TUCHMAN, MITCH. "Spielberg's Close Encounter." *Film Comment*, January–February 1978.

BLACKS AND WOMEN IN HOLLYWOOD

BOOKS

CRIPPS, T. R. *Black Film as Genre*. Bloomington: Indiana University Press, 1978.

SMITH, SHARON. *Women Who Make Movies*. New York: Hopkinson & Blake, 1975.

ARTICLES

DAVIS, SALLY OGLE. "The Struggle of Women Directors." *New York Times Magazine*, January 11, 1981.

WEAVER, HAROLD D., JR. "Black Filmmakers in Africa and America." *Sightlines*, Spring 1976.

For research on American filmmakers, two invaluable guides to periodicals are available in many public libraries: *Film Literature Index* and *International Index to Film Periodicals*.

For just keeping up, *American Film* (published by the American Film Institute, John F. Kennedy Center for the Performing Arts, Washington, D.C. 20556) and *Film Comment* (published by the Film Society of Lincoln Center, 140 W. 65 St., New York, N.Y. 10023) are very good sources of information about people and issues important in film today. Both magazines can be found in many public libraries and are available by subscription.

Index

159

About the Author

DIAN G. SMITH is a freelance writer with a master's degree in education from Harvard University. She is the author of *Careers in the Visual Arts: Talking with Professionals* and *Women in Finance*, and her articles have appeared in *Self, Glamour, 3-2-1 Contact* (Children's Television Workshop), the *Christian Science Monitor*, the *Chronicle of Higher Education*, and other national publications.

Her interest in film is long-standing and she comes by it naturally, for her great-aunt, Annie Warner Robins, was a sister of the Warner brothers.